P9-DCV-027

Archimedes

Mathematical Genius of the Ancient World

Mary Gow

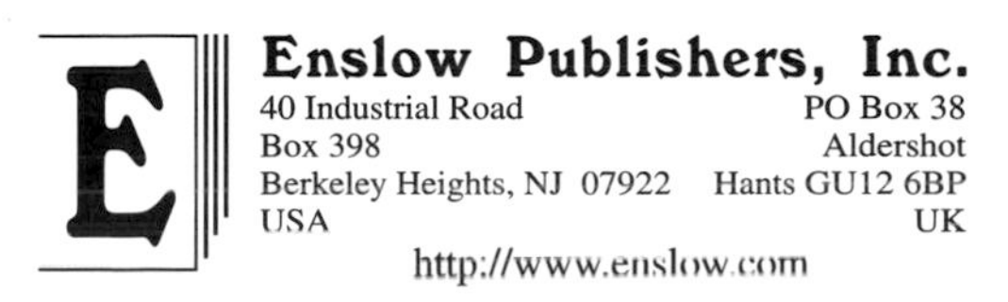

Library of Congress Cataloging-in-Publication Data

Gow, Mary.
Archimedes : mathematical genius of the ancient world / Mary Gow.
p. cm. — (Great minds of science)
Includes bibliographical references and index.
ISBN 0-7660-2502-0
1. Archimedes—Biography—Juvenile literature. 2. Mathematicians—Greece—Biography—Juvenile literature. 3. Mathematics, Ancient—Juvenile literature. 4. Mathematics—Study and teaching (Elementary) I. Title. II. Series.
QA29.A7G68 2005
510'.92—dc22

2004028480

Printed in the United States of America

10 9 8 7 6 5 4 3 2 1

To Our Readers:
We have done our best to make sure all Internet addresses in this book were active and appropriate when we went to press. However, the author and the publisher have no control over and assume no liability for the material available on those Internet sites or on other Web sites they may link to. Any comments or suggestions can be sent by e-mail to comments@enslow.com or to the address on the back cover.

Illustration Credits: ArtToday, Inc., pp. 13, 22, 51; Christie's Images, Inc. © 2005, p. 102; © The Trustees of The British Museum, p. 53; © Tom Davis, p. 45; Courtesy of Chris Rorres, pp. 91, 96, 106; Courtesy of Sam Meilach <www.meilach.com>, p. 17; Engraving of the Great Orrery inventory #93167, © Museum of the History of Science, Oxford, p. 86; Enslow Publishers, Inc., pp. 16, 62, 80; Renè Seindal, p. 24; Julius Goodman, pp. 65, 66, 75; Library of Congress, p. 8; Margaret Cowling Arts <www.arttour.com.au>, p. 19; National Oceanic and Atmospheric Administration/Department of Commerce, Image libr0073, treasures of the NOAA Library Collection, p. 30; National Oceanic and Atmospheric Administration/Department of Commerce, p. 56; Steve Hewitt, pp. 42, 82; University of Pennsylvania Museum of Archaeology and Anthropology T35-316, p. 35.

Cover Illustration: Courtesy of Sam Meilach <http://www.meilach.com> (background); Library of Congress (inset).

Contents

"Treasures of Scientific Knowledge"

"GIVE ME A PLACE TO STAND ON AND I will move the earth," the Greek mathematician, Archimedes, reportedly proclaimed over twenty-two centuries ago.[1] Archimedes knew that with certain simple machines a man could lift enormously heavy objects. According to the tale, King Hieron II was amazed by Archimedes' words. The king asked him to prove his claim by moving a great weight with little effort.

A large and heavy ship stood on the land. By one account, it was an enormous three-masted grain ship that had just been built and had not yet been dragged to the water. Moving the ship would normally require many men's labor. Archimedes set up equipment and connected ropes to the vessel. Finally, he sat down. In his hand, he held a pulley with a rope passing through it. When Archimedes pulled the rope, the ship began to move. It glided, wrote the ancient historian Plutarch, "as smoothly and evenly as if she had been in the sea."[2]

"From this day forth Archimedes is to be believed in everything he may say," King Hieron II reportedly exclaimed in astonishment.[3]

Archimedes' demonstration impressed the king, and today his achievements still inspire awe. In subjects from geometry to hydrostatics to mechanics, Archimedes made new discoveries. Imaginative and insightful, Archimedes tackled problems that were previously unsolved. With perseverance and genius he found solutions. Archimedes is considered one of the greatest mathematicians of all time. He is admired as a brilliant physicist, engineer, and inventor whose ideas and studies advanced human knowledge.

One discovery by this famous Greek thinker

is known as Archimedes' principle. Archimedes' principle explains why a block of wood floats in water but a block of steel of the same weight sinks. It explains why a steel ship can sail through the waves but the same steel in a different shape would drop to the ocean floor. Archimedes' principle explains buoyancy—the ability of objects to float.

Archimedes made many discoveries in mathematics—especially in geometry. Geometry is the branch of mathematics that deals with points, lines, planes, and figures. Circles, spheres, spirals, and other curved shapes fascinated Archimedes. He discovered how to measure the surface area of a sphere. He found the relationship between the volumes of spheres and cylinders of the same radius. He determined a good estimation for pi—the number that expresses the relationship between the circumference and diameter of a circle. Many geometry equations taught in schools today were first discovered by Archimedes.

Archimedes explained and proved the law of

No portraits of Archimedes from his lifetime still exist. This engraving of him was done many centuries after his death. It is the artist's impression of his appearance.

the lever. A lever is a simple machine that consists of a bar moving around a fixed point. Seesaws, crowbars, and even a foot kicking a ball are all examples of levers. Levers have an amazing ability to make it easier to lift or move objects. The law of the lever explains how weight or force applied to one end of a lever can be balanced with unequal weight at the other end of the lever.

Understanding mechanical principles like the law of the lever helped Archimedes design machines. He is credited with inventing the compound pulley and a water-moving machine called Archimedes' screw. Compound pulleys, like levers, can make it easier for a person to raise a heavy weight. Archimedes made ingenious models of the cosmos—the universe as it was understood in his time. The planets, moon, sun, and stars all moved in these models. Archimedes also used his mechanical knowledge to design weapons to defend his city, Syracuse. His war machines used levers and pulleys to hurl heavy rocks and snatch Roman ships from the sea.

Archimedes lived in the ancient Greek

city-state of Syracuse in the third century B.C. Syracuse stood on the southeastern coast of the island of Sicily in the Mediterranean Sea. With a fine harbor, a bustling business district, stately temples, and a massive theater, ancient Syracuse was known for its beauty and wealth.

From accounts written by ancient Greeks and Romans we know that Archimedes was famous in Syracuse and far beyond its borders. He was admired for his genius. He was known as a mathematician, but probably only a small group of ancient scholars understood his mathematical achievements. Most ancient writers were more impressed by his inventions. Many wrote glowing accounts about his weapons.

Stories about Archimedes were written for hundreds of years. Unfortunately, every ancient account about Archimedes that still exists was written after he died. It is impossible to prove which statements about him are accurate. For this reason, scholars feel that only a few details of Archimedes' life can be accepted as facts.[4] These facts are that Syracuse was his home, he spent time in Alexandria, Egypt, and he died in 212 B.C. Although the existing accounts cannot be proven, it does not mean that they are all untrue. Some may be accurate and others may be legends—stories based on true events.

Plutarch, a Greek historian and essayist, lived about 250 years after Archimedes. His writing combined historical facts, legends, and his own views.[5] Plutarch wrote a detailed account of the siege of Syracuse—an event at the end of Archimedes' life. In it he told of many of Archimedes' feats. Archimedes, said Plutarch, had a high spirit and a profound soul, and he possessed "treasures of scientific knowledge." He "placed his whole affection and ambition" in his studies.[6]

Plutarch claimed that Archimedes was sometimes so involved in his work that he forgot to eat or wash. At times, Plutarch said, he had to be "carried by absolute violence to bathe." Even then, he was so interested in his work that "he used to trace geometrical figures in the ashes of the fire, and diagrams in the oil on his body, being in a state of entire preoccupation."[7]

Although we have few verifiable facts about Archimedes' life, we know a great deal about his investigations and discoveries. Archimedes did not just think great thoughts, he wrote them down. Parts of thirteen of his books exist today. Several others disappeared over time.

Many of Archimedes' books are about geometry. *Measurement of the Circle*, *On Spirals,* and *On the Sphere and the Cylinder* are among his books that deal with curved figures. In these he lays out his theorems (or propositions). He carefully shows how he proves them to be true. In some he offers a glimpse of his excitement. "How many theorems in geometry which have seemed at first impracticable are in time successfully worked out!" he wrote enthusiastically in the introduction to *On Spirals.*[8]

Some of Archimedes' works reveal his playful side. In one book, *The Cattle Problem*, he challenged other mathematicians to calculate how many cattle were in a mythological herd in

This image of Archimedes moving Earth with a lever appeared in Mechanics *magazine in London in 1824.*

Sicily. This problem was finally solved in 1981. In *The Sand-Reckoner*, Archimedes set out to calculate the grains of sand needed to fill the entire universe. His real goal was to explore very large numbers.

A new chapter in our understanding of Archimedes was recently opened. In 1998 a book called the Archimedes Palimpsest sold for two million dollars. The book's handwritten pages contain the earliest existing copies of several of Archimedes' works. The palimpsest also includes some of his writing that was once believed lost forever.

Mystery, luck, and dedication have all factored in this unusual book's survival. The foresight and generosity of its new owner are now shaping its future. The present owner of the Archimedes Palimpsest is having the book studied and restored by a team of international scientists and mathematicians. Using tools of modern technology, they are reading words of Archimedes that have not been seen for centuries.

The Son of Phidias

TODAY, ARCHIMEDES' HOMETOWN OF Syracuse is known as Siracusa. This lovely city on the coast of Sicily still wraps around the splendid harbor that made it a great shipping center in ancient times. Places that Archimedes knew are landmarks there. Ruins of the Temple of Apollo stand in a busy neighborhood. The Temple of Athena's majestic white columns now support the roof of a Christian cathedral.

In Syracuse's immense Greek theater, visitors sit on cool, smooth limestone seats. Archimedes himself probably sat in these seats and watched plays. Near the theater are ruins of the Altar of

A map of Sicily and surrounding areas of note in Archimedes' lifetime.

Hieron, a massive stone structure more than six hundred feet long. The altar was built by Archimedes' king and was used to sacrifice animals as offerings to the Greek gods.

Although we have few details about Archimedes' life, we can form a picture of him by looking at the history of his city and the Greek culture of his time.

When Archimedes was born, Syracuse was already nearly five hundred years old. The city had been settled by Greeks in the eighth century B.C. The settlers made a wise choice for their new home. The island of Sicily had much rich farmland. Grain and other crops grew well there.

From their island's central location in the Mediterranean Sea, the Syracusans shipped grain,

The Greek theater in Syracuse. This massive amphitheater was cut from the rock in the hillside in the fifth century B.C. *King Hieron enlarged and improved the theater during Archimedes' lifetime.*

wool, pigs, cheese, pickled fish, and other goods to North Africa, Greece, and the Italian peninsula. Vast numbers of wooden ships with sails and long rows of oars docked in Syracuse's fine natural harbor. Syracuse prospered and for a time was the most powerful city in Europe.[1]

Syracuse was a Greek *polis* or city-state. In the ancient world there were many Greek city-states. Syracuse, Athens, and Sparta were among them. City-states were independent of each other. Each one had its own king or ruler. Although they were independent, city-states often formed alliances, agreeing to trade with each other or fight together in wars. A *polis* included the city center as well as surrounding farmland and villages.

Greek life was closely tied to Greek religion. The ancient Greeks believed myths about human-like gods and goddesses. These deities were identified with certain ideas and activities. Apollo was the god of arts and sciences. Athena was the goddess of war for just causes. She was also the goddess of law and wisdom. Greeks built temples to be the gods' dwelling places. Theaters were dedicated to the gods.

Belief in these gods was evident in Syracuse. The city's magnificent Temple of Athena stood on high ground above the harbor. Grand limestone columns lined the temple's sides. An enormous statue of Athena stood on the temple roof facing the harbor. In her hand she held a golden shield that reflected the sun.

Fishing boats docked in modern Syracuse.

Her blazing shield served as a beacon to ships at sea.[2]

Ancient Greeks celebrated many religious festivals. Like modern holidays, some were celebrated every year. The *Anthisteria* was a spring ceremony dedicated to the god Dionysius. Dionysius was the god of the grapevine. Wine made from grapes was part of the daily Greek diet. At the Anthesteria, everyone in a community three years of age or older drank wine together to honor Dionysius.[3]

Other religious celebrations occurred less frequently. Every four years, Greek athletes traveled to the sacred city of Olympia to compete in games. With competitions in running, wrestling, throwing, and other sports, the Olympics honored Zeus, the most powerful of the Greek gods.

Animal offerings and feasts were features of Greek celebrations. Oxen, goats, sheep, and other animals were sacrificed to the gods. The animals were killed in a ritual directed by a Greek priest. Then they were roasted. The

Greeks offered the animals' bones and innards to the gods. The people celebrating the festival ate the tastier portions of meat.

Greek religion would have been part of Archimedes' life. When he was five days old, his father probably carried him around the hearth in their home. This ritual was called the *Amphidromia*. The Amphidromia honored Hestia, the goddess of the hearth.[4] As a boy, Archimedes may have participated in festivals dedicated to the god Apollo. Boys sang and carried branches decorated with dangling fruit and wool in some of Apollo's celebrations.[5] Archimedes could have known the athletes who represented Syracuse in the Olympics. He would have feasted at festivals when oxen and sheep were sacrificed.

Scholars think that Archimedes was born in Syracuse around 287 B.C. His birth date was determined from stories about his death. Archimedes was killed in 212 B.C. According to one account, he was seventy-five years old when he died. Seventy-five years before 212 B.C. is 287 B.C.

For many centuries nothing was known about

In ancient Greek mythology Athena was the goddess of wisdom, law and order, and war for just causes.

Archimedes' parents. In the late 1800s a noted scholar, F. Blass, suggested that Archimedes' father was named Phidias. Blass knew a perplexing phrase in one of Archimedes' books, *The Sand-Reckoner*. Translators with superb knowledge of ancient Greek could not figure out what Archimedes meant by one group of words. Blass saw that if one letter was changed, the phrase had meaning. With this change, the Greek words could be translated as "our father Phidias."[6] Archimedes' works were copied over and over by hand in ancient times. One letter could easily have been copied incorrectly.

The reference to Phidias is in a section where Archimedes was writing about astronomers and their estimates of the size of the universe. From Archimedes' words and Blass's skillful interpretation, scholars now believe that Archimedes' father was an astronomer named Phidias. Ancient astronomers studied the movements of the heavens. Many were capable mathematicians. Phidias may have taught his son mathematics and inspired his love of science.

Besides his father's teaching, Archimedes probably had a formal education. Many boys in ancient Greece studied in schools. Girls did not. Boys' schooling started at age seven. They learned Greek grammar and memorized poems. Their studies included literature and music.

The altar of Hieron II was built by Syracuse's king during Archimedes' lifetime. According to one ancient source, over 450 oxen could be sacrificed on this altar at one time.

Boys played sports and practiced running and throwing the discus.

When Archimedes was a young man an event changed his city and his life. Hieron II became king of Syracuse. As king, Hieron kept Syracuse at peace through challenging times.

During the early third century B.C. differences between Rome and Carthage were erupting into war. Rome and Carthage were both great powers. Both were trying to expand their territories. Their efforts resulted in three long, bloody conflicts called the Punic Wars. Syracuse's location between them put the city in peril. Rome was located on the Italian peninsula, north of Sicily. Carthage, on the coast of North Africa, was south of the island.

Hieron became king of Syracuse in about 270 B.C. In the war between Carthage and Rome, he at first sided with Carthage. After a short time Hieron changed his position and signed a treaty with Rome. Under the treaty Syracuse sent supplies and grain to the Romans. Romans and Carthaginians fought each other for more than twenty years in the first Punic War. Syracuse stayed out of their conflict. Because of Hieron's treaty, Syracuse enjoyed peace and prosperity.

According to Plutarch, Archimedes was a "friend and near relation" of Hieron.[7] Several stories tell how Archimedes solved problems or did favors for the king. Archimedes reportedly exposed a fraud for Hieron. Several accounts tell of fabulous weapons he designed at Hieron's request. Archimedes' own words support the idea that he and Hieron were related. Archimedes began his book *The Sand Reckoner* with a friendly note to Hieron's son, Gelon. Whether or not King Hieron II and Archimedes were related cannot be proved. However, clearly there were many ties between them. Because of Hieron's leadership, Archimedes lived for years in a city that was at peace. With peace, leisure, and the king's interest, Archimedes could dedicate his life to his studies.

3 Alexandria and Mathematics

ALTHOUGH ARCHIMEDES LIVED MOST OF his life in Syracuse, another great ancient city helped shape him as a mathematician. This city, Alexandria, also played an important role in preserving Archimedes' works for future generations. Alexandria was one of the greatest centers of learning of the ancient world. Archimedes and other thinkers who advanced the fields of mathematics, astronomy, medicine, and geography studied there.

Alexandria stood nine hundred miles across the Mediterranean Sea from Syracuse. It was situated at the mouth of the Nile River in Egypt.

The Greek conqueror Alexander the Great founded the city and named it for himself about forty-five years before Archimedes was born. Alexandria was a Greek city governed by Greek rulers.

By the time Archimedes was a young man, Alexandria was an exciting intellectual metropolis. It was a vibrant academic center because of its rulers. These rulers were kings in the Ptolemy family. Ptolemys would rule Egypt for nearly 250 years. Ptolemy I, the first of the dynasty, was a general who served Alexander the Great. After Alexander died, Ptolemy I became king of Egypt.

King Ptolemy I launched several impressive projects in Alexandria. His works were continued by his son, Ptolemy II. This father and son built a magnificent lighthouse at Alexandria's harbor entrance. The lighthouse stood four hundred feet high.[1] It was admired as one of the seven wonders of the ancient world. Ptolemy I also built the *Mouseion*, a temple dedicated to the Muses. The Muses were Greek goddesses of memory, song, music, history, astronomy, poetry, and more. Our modern word *museum* comes from the word *muse*.

The Mouseion was far more than a temple. The Mouseion had laboratories, lecture rooms, a zoo, and accommodations.[2] It was in many ways like a modern university—a place where learning is cultivated and knowledge is preserved. Many poets, historians, mathematicians, scientists, and other scholars flocked to Alexandria to study and to teach.

Near the Mouseion, possibly even attached to it, was Alexandria's great library. This was not the first library in the world—other kings had libraries. However, this library was different. Through the efforts of the Ptolemys, the library was a treasury of Greek culture.[3] Any Greek writing that was valued was collected there. Homer's epic poems, Herodotus's histories, Aristotle's natural philosophy, and thousands of other works were in Alexandria's collection. The library shelves also held many ancient works that are now lost forever.

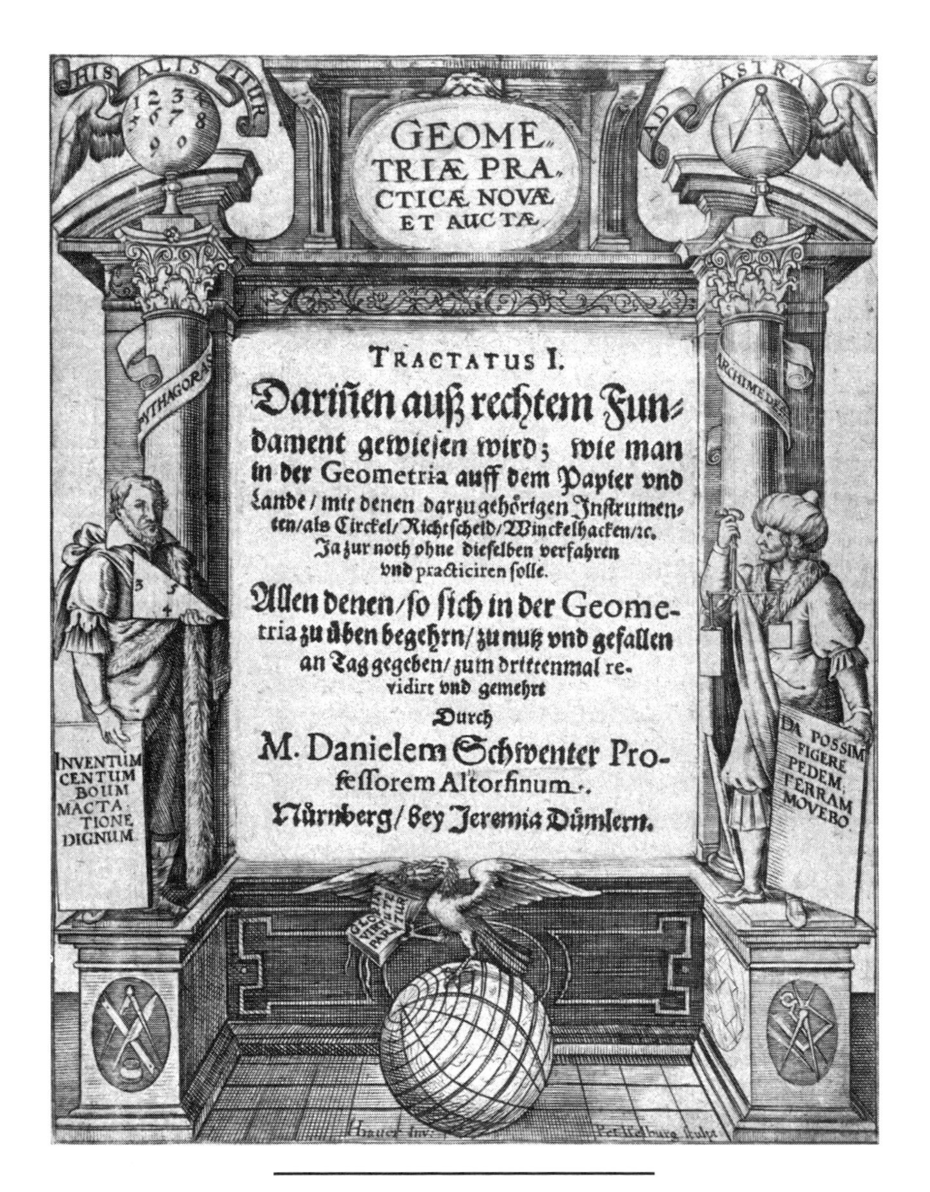

GEOMETRIÆ PRACTICÆ NOVÆ ET AUCTÆ

TRACTATUS I.

Dariñen auß rechtem Fundament gewiesen wird; wie man in der Geometria auff dem Papier vnd Lande / mit denen darzu gehörigen Instrumenten / als Circkel / Richtscheid / Winckelhacken / etc. Ja zur noth ohne dieselben verfahren vnd practiciren solle.

Allen denen / so sich in der Geometria zu üben begehrn / zu nutz vnd gefallen an Tag gegeben / zum drittenmal revidirt vnd gemehrt

Durch

M. Danielem Schwenter Professorem Altorfinum.

Nürnberg / bey Jeremia Dümlern.

Title page of a geometry book published in 1641. Pythagoras is pictured on the left holding a right triangle. Archimedes is on the right holding a scale balanced with two blocks of different sizes. The blocks balance because the larger block is closer to the fulcrum and the smaller block is proportionally farther away.

The Ptolemys were enthusiastic collectors. When ships docked in Alexandria they were searched for books. Any works found on them were borrowed and copied. The copies were added to the library collection.[4] Ptolemy I reportedly borrowed manuscripts of Greek plays from the city of Athens. Borrowing them, he had to pay a deposit of fifteen gold talents, a huge sum of money. Athens would return his money when he returned their manuscripts. Ptolemy had the plays copied. Then he forfeited the gold and sent the copies back to Athens. He kept the originals in his library.[5]

The books on Alexandria's shelves looked different from books in modern libraries. Alexandria's books were rolls of papyrus. Papyrus, a tall reedy plant, flourished in Egypt. Our word *paper* is derived from *papyrus*. Ancient Egyptians discovered that papyrus could be made into a fine writing material. The reeds were cut, laid across each other, glued, and pressed into smooth long sheets. Sheets of papyrus were sometimes more than twenty feet long.

Ancient Egyptians began writing on papyrus around 2,000 B.C. In the fifth century B.C., ancient Greeks began recording their works on papyrus, too. Prior to that time, the Greeks passed on much of their knowledge orally—by telling stories over and over. They wrote on wooden boards, wax tablets, and pieces of pottery.[6] With papyrus sheets they could keep written copies of their poems, plays, and ideas.

Alexandria's library was filled with long sheets of papyrus. The sheets were stored as rolls. The rolls were sometimes kept in pottery tubes. Papyrus was fragile. The sheets tore easily. They decayed if they were damp. When important papyrus manuscripts were damaged, they were copied onto new rolls.

Under Ptolemy II, Alexandria's library reached extraordinary proportions. In 260 B.C., when Archimedes was around twenty-seven years old, the collection numbered 400,000 rolls. Some works required more than one roll. About 90,000 distinct works were there. A second Alexandrian library held another 40,000 works.[7]

We do not know exactly when Archimedes went to Alexandria. However, we do know that the city was already a center for mathematics—especially the study of geometry. The word *geometry* comes from ancient Greek. Geometry means "measure of the earth." Some geometry was known before the Greeks. Ancient Egyptians knew how to measure the area of fields. They had a practical understanding of geometry that they used to build pyramids and other impressive structures.

Ancient Greeks took geometry in a new direction. They began to logically deduce geometric facts. They proved that certain rules were universal. Pythagoras, who lived more than two hundred years before Archimedes, was one of the first great Greek mathematicians. Pythagoras proved that the angles of a triangle add up to 180 degrees. He proved the Pythagorean theorem. The Pythagorean theorem states the relationship between the lengths of the sides of a right triangle.

In the years between Pythagoras and

Archimedes, there were many other Greek mathematicians. One of the greatest was Euclid. Euclid spent years in Alexandria. He reportedly died there when Archimedes was about twenty-two years old. Archimedes learned from Euclid's books but apparently the two mathematicians never met. Euclid did not make original discoveries. He explained other mathematicians' discoveries. Euclid wrote thirteen books known as *The Elements*. *The Elements* is considered the greatest mathematical textbook ever written. *The Elements* is still used to teach geometry today.

In *The Elements*, Euclid began with certain definitions and universally accepted assumptions called postulates. "A line is a breadthless length," and "An obtuse angle is an angle greater than a right angle," were among his definitions. The postulates included statements like "All right angles are equal."[8] From these accepted facts, Euclid proved ideas called propositions. His propositions describe properties of squares, triangles, circles and various three-dimensional

The Euclid Papyrus. A geometry proposition and a diagram from Euclid's Elements is written on this fragment of papyrus. The fragment is believed to date from about 100 A.D. *The proposition is written in the ancient Greek language.*

figures. Euclid presented his proof of these propositions logically. Students could follow his ideas and reach the same conclusions.

Archimedes and other mathematicians used Euclid's proofs as models for their own investigations. Archimedes postulates and propositions are presented in the same way as Euclid's. Because he knew Euclid's geometry,

Archimedes was able to go further and make new discoveries.

The achievements of Pythagoras, Euclid, Archimedes, and other ancient mathematicians are impressive. They are almost unbelievable when we consider the awkward Greek number system they used. Greek numbers were different from ours. Greeks expressed numbers with the twenty-seven letters of their alphabet. They had no symbol for 0. With their number system they could write fractions but not decimal places.[9]

Addition and subtraction were not too complicated for them. Doing these calculations, they lined up the letters according to values. Multiplication and division, however, were cumbersome. The highest number symbol in the Greek system was 10,000, called a *myriad*. The highest number that could be written was a *myriad myriads* or 100,000,000. This limitation frustrated Archimedes. Eventually he figured out his own way to expand the system.

We do not know how long Archimedes stayed in Alexandria, but we do know that he stayed in contact with mathematicians there for many years. "Archimedes to Dositheus greeting," are the opening words to five of his books. "In this book, I have set forth and send you the proofs of the remaining theorems not included in what I sent you before," he wrote to Dositheus in *On Conoids and Spheroids.*[10] Archimedes sent many of his important mathematical investigations to scholars in Alexandria. He started several of his works with a short letter about his discoveries. Then he presented his mathematical theorems and investigations.

Archimedes sent his geometry to at least three scholars in Alexandria—Conon, Dositheus, and Eratosthenes. Conon was a mathematician and astronomer whom Archimedes valued as a friend. After Conon died, Archimedes began corresponding with Dositheus. Archimedes wrote that Dositheus was "versed in geometry," but little else is known about the man who received the original copies of so many of Archimedes' discoveries.[11]

Eratosthenes, the third scholar to correspond

with Archimedes, remains famous for his many remarkable achievements. Eratosthenes was a mathematician, geographer, and astronomer. He served as head librarian in Alexandria. Eratosthenes wrote books about geography, theater, and mathematics. Twenty-two centuries ago, Eratosthenes measured the circumference of the earth with amazing accuracy. Eratosthenes and other ancient Greeks knew that the earth was a sphere. For his calculations, Eratosthenes measured shadows cast when the sun was at its highest point in the sky. Eratosthenes also calculated the distance from the earth to the sun, mapped the known world, and developed a calendar that included leap years.

Eratosthenes, Conon, and Dositheus were all mathematicians who could understand Archimedes' discoveries. Besides learning from his investigations themselves, they could teach his discoveries to others. Being in Alexandria, they also helped assure that his works were copied and preserved for future generations.

The Law of the Lever

A BOOK CALLED *ON THE EQUILIBRIUM OF Planes or the Centres of Gravity of Planes* is believed to be one of Archimedes' earliest works. In it, he showed his genius for seeing familiar things in a new way.

Since distant prehistory, humankind has used tools to make jobs easier. One of these, a simple machine called a lever, can make it easier to lift heavy weights or pry objects loose. With a lever, a person can raise a boulder, log, or an automobile that is many times the person's own weight. Levers are such basic tools that chimpanzees living in the wild use them to open insect nests. A lever consists of a rigid bar moving around a fixed point. The bar may be a board, a stick, a bone or another inflexible object. The fixed point is called the *fulcrum*.

To explain the lever, Archimedes approached the device as a mathematical problem. Greek mathematicians used assumptions that were accepted as facts to logically prove that certain rules in geometry were universal. Archimedes followed these same steps. He used accepted facts of geometry to prove a universal principle that describes the fundamental nature of the lever. This was an important leap in the development of science. Archimedes showed that the performance of some physical objects, like the lever, could be predicted with mathematics. The principle that Archimedes proved mathematically is called *the law of the lever*.

The law of the lever states how to balance a lever. By doing this, it provides a way to calculate a lever's mechanical advantage. *Mechanical advantage* is how many pounds of weight may be moved by a pound of force. The lever and other simple tools work by trading distance for force. In the case of the lever, if the weight that needs to be moved is close to the fulcrum, it can be moved with less force. However, by being close to the fulcrum, it does not move a very great distance. If the weight is farther from the fulcrum, greater force is required to move it, but the weight moves a greater distance.

In his book, Archimedes did not use the words *lever, force,* or *mechanical advantage*. He explained this principle in terms of equilibrium and planes. *Equilibrium* means a state of balance or equality. A *plane* is a flat surface. In geometry, a plane is two-dimensional.

We can see Archimedes' law of the lever applied in the physical world with the help of a playground seesaw. A seesaw is a lever. The long board people sit on is the seesaw's rigid bar. The point around which the board pivots is its fulcrum. Imagine that two students who weigh 100 pounds each are at the playground with a teacher who weighs 200 pounds. With the assistance of the students and the teacher, we can follow some of Archimedes' steps in proving the law of the lever. We can also use the law of the lever to predict when the students and teacher will balance.

Archimedes began his book with certain postulates. He wrote, "I postulate the following:

A playground seesaw is a lever. A lighter student can balance a heavier one if the lighter student sits a greater distance from the fulcrum.

Equal weights at equal distances are in equilibrium."[1] In other words, equal weights on a lever at equal distances from the fulcrum will balance. The two 100-pound students can balance the seesaw if they sit on opposite ends of the board and if each student is at the same distance from the fulcrum. If the two students sit on one end and the 200-pound teacher sits at the same distance from the fulcrum on the other end, they will also balance.

Archimedes continued, "Equal weights at unequal distances are not in equilibrium but incline toward the weight which is at greater distance."[2] Again, imagine the two students on the seesaw. If one student stays at the end of the seesaw but the other moves closer to the fulcrum the seesaw tips. The student closer to the fulcrum will be lifted up from the ground.

Archimedes used accepted facts about balancing equal and unequal weights to prove several propositions. He stated two propositions together as the law of the lever. In Archimedes' words, "Two magnitudes whether commensurable or incommensurable balance at distances reciprocally proportional to their magnitudes."[3] Another way of saying this is that if the distance from the fulcrum times the weight of the object on one side of the lever equals the distance times the weight of the object on the other side, the lever will balance.

Consider the seesaw again. Imagine a 200-pound teacher and a 100-pound student sitting on the seesaw. If they sit at opposite ends of the seesaw and each one is the same distance from the fulcrum, the teacher will be on the ground and the student in the air. However, if the teacher changes position and sits at a point half the student's distance from the fulcrum, they will balance.

The law of the lever is mathematically stated D1W1 = D2W2. In this equation, "D" stands for distance from the fulcrum and "W" represents weight. The equation means that a lever will balance if one object's distance from the fulcrum multiplied by the object's weight is equal to

This model of Earth being moved by a lever was inspired by Archimedes' quote, "Give me a place to stand on and I will move the earth." This "Earth" could be moved by one person's effort. Also, a person could sit inside the model for a ride.

a second object's distance from the fulcrum times its weight.

Imagine the student and teacher as the two objects. Suppose the 100 pound student sat eight feet from the fulcrum. Eight times 100 equals 800. To balance the lever, the 200 pound teacher must sit four feet from the fulcrum, because 4 times 200 also equals 800. If the teacher sits anywhere else on the lever, the two will not balance.

Understanding the law of the lever makes it possible to calculate the weight or force needed to balance or move another weight. For example, suppose a 100-pound student wanted to balance a 1,000 pound crate. The student and crate would balance if the crate was on the lever and one foot from the fulcrum and the student was ten feet from the fulcrum on the opposite side. The student's 100 pounds multiplied by ten feet equals 1,000. The crate's 1,000 pounds multiplied by one foot equals 1,000. The two weights being equal would balance. If the student wished to raise the crate, the student could move farther from the fulcrum or add additional weight to her side of the lever.

Knowledge of the law of the lever makes it possible to calculate how long a lever is needed to move a weight and also how much force or weight is required to move it. Archimedes used his understanding of mechanical advantage to design machines that threw spears, moved heavy rocks, and lifted ships from the sea. Archimedes' understanding of mechanical advantage is the basis of the story about moving the king's ship. It is also the foundation of his claim "Give me a place to stand on and I can move the world."

5

"Eureka!" Archimedes' Principle

"AS FOR ARCHIMEDES, ALTHOUGH IN HIS limitless wisdom he discovered many wonderful things, nonetheless, of all of them, one in particular . . . seems to convey his boundless ingenuity," wrote Vitruvius, beginning the most famous story about Archimedes.[1] Vitruvius was a Roman architect and engineer who lived during the first century B.C. His account is the oldest known version of this enduring tale.

King Hieron II, explained Vitruvius, "decided . . . to dedicate a votive crown of gold to the immortal gods."[2] Ancient Greeks often gave gifts to the gods to express their thanks or show respect for them. The crown probably looked like a wreath of entwined branches. Hieron would have put it in a temple, perhaps on the head of a sculpture of Zeus or another god. Hieron hired a goldsmith to make the wreath. He weighed out the exact amount of gold that was to be used and gave it to the craftsman.

After he received the finished crown Hieron became suspicious. The crown's weight was exactly the same as the gold he had given the craftsman. However, Hieron suspected that the goldsmith had mixed silver with the gold. Silver cost far less than gold. By looking at the crown it was impossible to detect a fraud. The metals may have been cleverly blended or the silver may have been concealed under the gold. Hieron asked Archimedes to investigate.

"Now Archimedes, once he had charge of this matter, chanced to go to the baths," explained Vitruvius.[3] In ancient Greece, men bathed in public baths. When Archimedes "stepped into the tub, he noticed that however much he immersed his body in it, that much water spilled over the sides."[4] "When the reason for this occurrence came clear to him, he did not hesitate," wrote Vitruvius. "In a transport of joy he leapt out of the tub, and as he rushed home naked, he let one and all know that he had truly found what he had been looking for—because as he ran he shouted over and over in Greek 'I found it! I found it!' (Eureka! Eureka!)"[5]

The story of Archimedes' unclothed dash through the streets of Syracuse has been told through the centuries. Scholars doubt its accuracy, but the tale still vividly captures the excitement of scientific discovery.[6] Archimedes' exuberance was inspired by his discovery of a method to solve the king's problem. As the bath water overflowed, Archimedes observed that a body immersed in water displaces a volume of water equal to its own volume. This observation showed him how to determine whether the king had been cheated.

To test King Hieron's crown, Archimedes got quantities of gold and silver exactly equal to the

An artist's impression of Archimedes in the bath. Note the crown on the floor, alongside the tub.

weight of the crown. He filled a large bowl to the brim with water. He lowered the silver into the water. Archimedes measured the amount of water that overflowed when the silver was immersed. "He discovered that a certain weight of silver corresponded to a certain measure of water," wrote Vitruvius.[7] Archimedes filled the bowl again and immersed the gold. When he measured the overflowed water, he found that less water had overflowed. The gold displaced less water than the silver of exactly the same weight.

Archimedes filled the bowl for a third test. This time he immersed the crown. When he measured the overflowed water, he saw that more water was needed to replace the crown than to replace the gold. Archimedes had found his answer. "Because there was more water in the crown's place than in the place of the mass of gold, he detected . . . the mixture of the silver in the crown," explained Vitruvius.[8] So the king was correct—he had been cheated.

Through these tests, Archimedes observed that two objects of exactly the same weight displaced different amounts of water. This observation relates to the *density* of substances. Density is expressed as how much weight is in a certain volume of a substance. A cubic foot is a volume one foot long, one foot wide, and one foot high. A cubic foot of silver weighs 653 pounds. Silver's density is 653 pounds per cubic foot. A cubic foot of pure gold is exactly the same size as the cubic foot of silver: one foot high, wide, and deep. A cubic foot of gold weighs 1,204 pounds. A one pound block of gold is about half the size of a one pound block of silver.

The crown that King Hieron ordered from the goldsmith may have resembled this gold oak leaf crown made during the fourth century B.C.

Archimedes' existing books do not mention the king's crown. Archimedes did, however, make important discoveries that relate to this story. He is considered the founder of the study of *hydrostatics*. Hydrostatics is the branch of science that deals with liquids at rest. Archimedes's book *On Floating Bodies* is the earliest known work about hydrostatics.

One of Archimedes's most famous discoveries is presented in *On Floating Bodies*. His discovery explains why some objects float but others sink. Archimedes' principle states that a body immersed in a fluid is buoyed up by a force equal to the weight of the displaced fluid.

Buoyancy is an object's apparent loss of weight in a fluid. Water and other liquids are fluids. Gases are too. In *On Floating Bodies*, Archimedes explained why a stone sinks in water but a piece of dry wood floats. He revealed why a person can lift a heavier object under the water than out of it.

You may have observed Archimedes' principle when you were swimming. Did you ever notice that you could carry a person in the water you could not lift on land? You can lift them because underwater they are lighter by the weight of the water that their body has displaced. Water weighs about sixty-two pounds per cubic foot. When you lift a person in the water, for each cubic foot of their submerged volume, they feel about sixty-two pounds lighter.

In *On Floating Bodies*, Archimedes wrote about objects of the same weight as a fluid, lighter than a fluid, and heavier than a fluid. In his words, solids "of equal weight with the fluid will sink down in the fluid until the surfaces no longer project above that of the fluid and they will not be driven down any further."[9] This principle can be observed with a water balloon. A balloon filled with water weighs almost exactly the same as the surrounding water in a tub or pool. In a pool of water, the balloon sinks below the surface but remains suspended instead of sinking to the bottom.

Regarding lighter objects, Archimedes wrote, "one which is lighter than the fluid, when thrown into the fluid, will not sink down

Archimedes' principle explains why a ship floats. The weight of the water displaced by the hull of this ship is equal to the weight of the ship itself—including the steel in its frame, its equipment, crew, the air, and everything else inside it.

altogether, but a portion of it will project above the surface of the fluid."[10] A piece of dry maple wood weighs less than water of the same volume. If the maple log is thrown into a lake, the log will sink until the water displaced by the immersed portion of the log is equal to the total weight of the log.

Finally Archimedes wrote, "Solids heavier than the fluid when thrown into the fluid, will be driven down as far as they can sink, and they will be lighter in the fluid by the weight of a portion of the fluid having the same volume as the solid."[11] In other words, a rock thrown into the water will sink to the bottom. If it was weighed there, it would weigh less than above the surface. Its weight would be reduced by the volume of the water it displaced.

From Archimedes' writing, we can understand why a solid block of steel sinks. Steel is heavier than water. Why, then, does a steel ship float? A ship floats because the total volume of the ship weighs less than an equal volume of water. A ship's hull when viewed from the end looks like a "U." The hull is not a solid piece of steel, but a shell of steel. The steel is distributed over a larger area when it is in the shape of a U than when it is in a solid block. Inside the U, the ship may carry cargo and a crew. It also usually has a large amount of air inside it. The total weight of the steel, cargo, crew, and air all presses down into the water through that U. As long as the total weight of the ship, cargo, crew, and air is less than the weight of an equal volume of water, the ship will float. The ship settles into the water at a level where the weight of the displaced water is equal to the weight of the ship.

Circles and Spheres

"IT IS NOT POSSIBLE TO FIND IN ALL geometry more difficult and intricate questions or more simple and lucid explanations," wrote the Greek historian Plutarch about Archimedes' mathematics. Plutarch said that once you saw one of Archimedes' investigations, "you immediately believe you would have discovered it; by so smooth and so rapid a path he leads you to the conclusion required."[1]

Archimedes wrote more about geometry than about any other subject. Many of his books present his discoveries about circles, spirals, spheres, and other figures bounded by curved lines and surfaces. *Measurement of a Circle, On the Sphere and Cylinder, On Conoids and Sphroids, On Spirals*, and *Quadrature of the Parabola* are the titles of some of Archimedes' works dealing with curved figures. In these books, Archimedes stated his theorems or propositions—the ideas he planned to prove. He also showed his investigations—the proof of his discoveries.

One of Archimedes' most famous calculations dealt with circles. Before Archimedes, other ancient Greeks studied circles. They knew that there was a constant relationship between the circumference and diameter of a circle. The *diameter* is a line across a circle passing through the circle's center point. The *circumference* is the line around a circle. The ratio that expresses the relationship between the circumference and diameter is known as *pi*. It is expressed by the Greek letter for *p* (π).

To understand pi, envision a string that is exactly the size of a circle. How many times could that string cover the diameter of the circle? The string would cover the diameter a little more than three times. Whether a circle is enormous or tiny, the ratio between its circumference and the diameter is always pi. Pi is a constant—its value is always the same. Besides circles, pi is used to calculate the volume and surface area of spheres, cylinders, and cones.

Archimedes calculated the value of pi in his book *Measurement of a Circle*. As with his other work, Archimedes proved his proposition about the value of pi by building on other known mathematical truths. This knowledge included how to calculate the perimeter of polygons. A *polygon* is a figure bounded by straight lines. Triangles, squares, and pentagons are all polygons. The perimeter is the figure's outer boundary.

Archimedes investigated pi by drawing a polygon inside a circle. All of the angles of the polygon touched the circle. He drew another polygon with the same number of sides just outside of the circle. All of its line segments touched the circle. Using his knowledge of triangles, Archimedes developed a mathematical formula to calculate the perimeters of the polygons. His calculations showed that pi was larger than the number found from the inner polygon, but smaller than the number derived from the outer polygon. Finally he had 96-sided polygons both inside and outside the circle. From these two figures, he derived his value for pi.

"The circumference of any circle is three times the diameter and exceeds it by less than

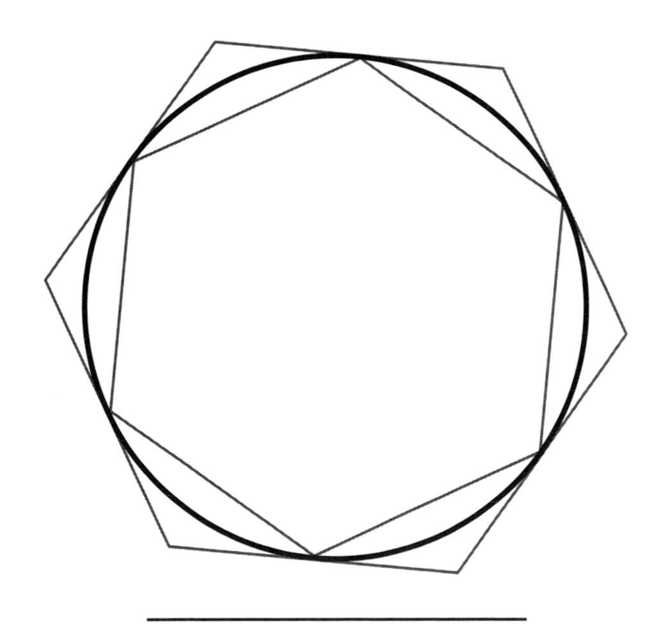

Archimedes discovered that he could calculate the value of pi (π) by calculating the perimeter of polygons inside and outside of a circle, as illustrated above. The greater the number of sides of the polygons, the more accurate the calculation would be.

one seventh of the diameter and more than ten-seventy-oneths," wrote Archimedes.[2] This can be stated that pi is smaller than $3\frac{1}{7}$ but greater than $3\frac{10}{71}$. Using decimals, Archimedes' calculation showed that pi is less than 3.1428 and more than 3.1408. Today, we know that the first ten digits of pi are 3.141592653.

Twenty-two centuries after Archimedes, mathematicians still study pi. Pi is an *irrational number*. An irrational number cannot be expressed as a fraction of two whole numbers. Using computers, pi has been calculated to more than 1.24 trillion decimal places. No pattern has been found in the sequence of decimal digits. Some people memorize the beginning of pi. In February 1995, twenty-one-year-old Hiroyuki Goto set a world record for pi memorization. In a television studio in Tokyo, Japan, Goto recited the first 42,195 digits of pi in nine hours. Reciting all the known digits of pi at a rate of five digits per second would take more than 7,858 years.

Besides calculating a good approximation of pi, Archimedes proved many other theorems about curved figures. One of these discoveries was how to calculate the surface area of a sphere. Archimedes stated this proposition in *On the Sphere and Cylinder*.

"The surface of any sphere," wrote Archimedes, "is equal to four times that of its greatest circle."[3] Imagine a globe of the world. Suppose you wanted to know how much surface area was on that globe. A great circle is any circle that divides the sphere into equal halves. The globe could be divided in half by any plane that passed through its center point. It can be divided in half on the line of the equator. The area of the flat circle on half of the globe would be the area of the greatest circle. Archimedes showed that if you multiply that area by four that is the surface area of the sphere.

Archimedes discovered the relationship between the surface area of spheres and cylinders of the same diameter and height. He found that the same relationship was true for the volumes of spheres and cylinders. A *sphere* is a solid figure in which all surface points are

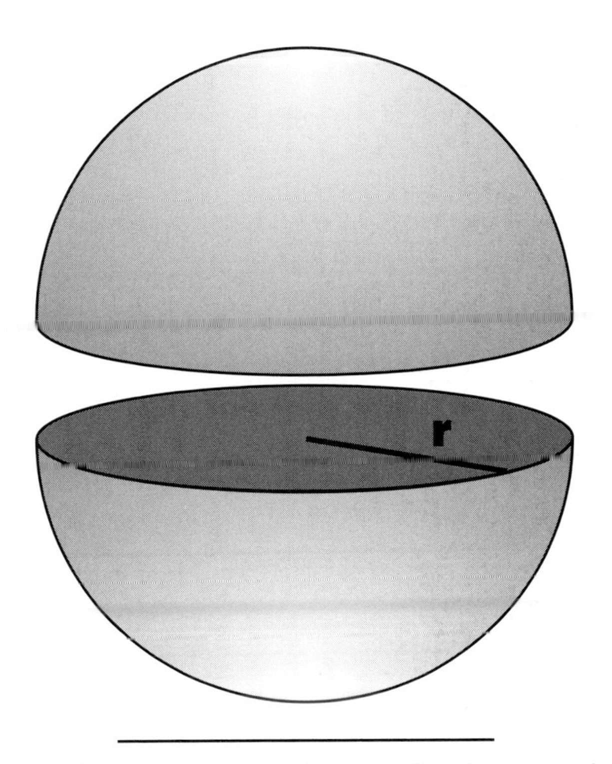

Archimedes discovered that the surface area of a sphere is equal to four times the area of its greatest circle. A circle's radius (r) is the distance from its center point to its perimeter.

at an equal distance from the center point. A round ball is a sphere. A *cylinder* is another solid figure. A cylinder has two identical circular bases that are parallel to each other. Soda cans are cylinders.

"Any cylinder whose base is equal to the greatest circle of those in the sphere and whose height is equal to the diameter, is itself half as large as again the sphere and its surface is half as large again as the surface of the sphere," wrote Archimedes.[4]

To get a picture of this proposition, imagine a can of tennis balls. Now imagine a small can exactly the right size for just one ball. Archimedes' discovery shows the relationship

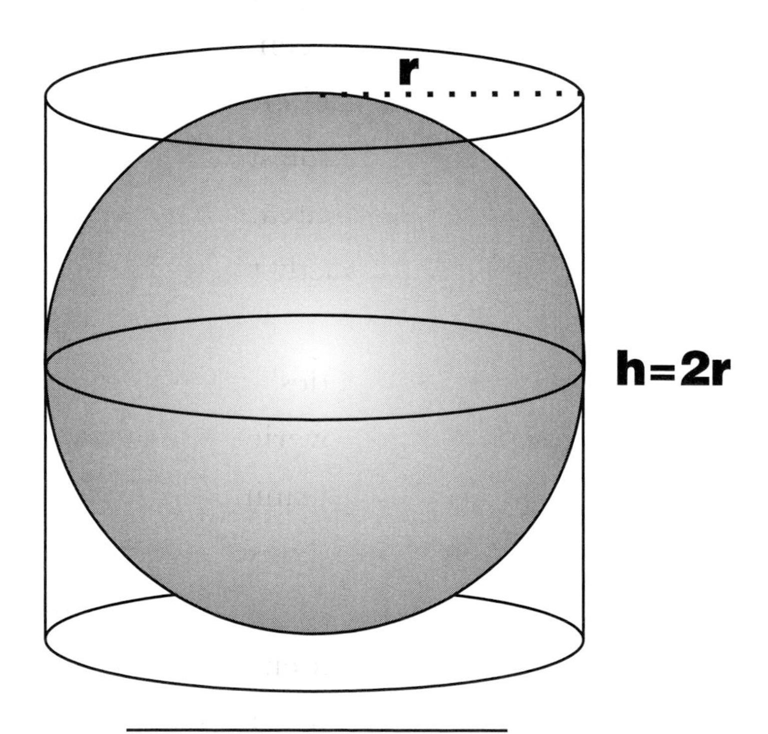

Archimedes discovered that the surface area of a sphere is exactly two thirds that of a cylinder of the same radius and height. The volume of a sphere is also two thirds the volume of a cylinder of the same radius and height.

between the volume of the tennis ball and the can. If the diameter of the sphere and cylinder are the same, the volume of the sphere would be exactly two thirds that of the cylinder. Another way of saying this is that the volume of the cylinder is three halves the volume of the sphere.

Archimedes discovered that the same relationship exists between the surface area of the two figures. In other words, the curved surface of the can plus the surfaces at its top and bottom add up to one area. The curved surface of the tennis ball is exactly two thirds as large as the surface of the can.

Of all of Archimedes' great mathematical achievements, his discoveries about spheres and cylinders had special meaning for him. Plutarch explained that Archimedes asked "his friends and relations" to place a monument on his tomb with a sphere and cylinder. He requested that it be inscribed with the ratio between their volumes and areas that he had discovered.[5]

Math at Play

"THERE ARE SOME, KING GELON, WHO think that the number of grains of sand is infinite. I mean not only of the sand which is present in Syracuse and the rest of Sicily, but also that which is found all over the world. . . . Others, indeed, do not assume that it is infinite, but they think that no such large expressible number exists."[1] Archimedes wrote those words as the introduction to his work *The Sand Reckoner*. King Gelon was the son of King Hieron II.

Besides Archimedes' books about geometry, levers, and buoyancy, he wrote several other works. Two of these, *The Sand Reckoner* and *The*

Cattle Problem, dealt with very large numbers. *The Stomachion* was a puzzle that required the reader to piece together geometric shapes. All three of these works have a playful side. They are also all mathematically challenging. They seem to show that Archimedes had fun devising and tackling very difficult problems.

Archimedes' challenge in *The Sand Reckoner* was to calculate the number of grains of sand required to fill the universe. The purpose of the problem was not really to know the actual number of grains of sand. Archimedes wanted a way to express a huge number. The largest number in the Greek number system was a myriad myriads, or 100,000,000. Archimedes wanted to be able to express much greater sums.

Archimedes offered a glimpse of the astronomy of his time in the introduction to *The Sand Reckoner*. The cosmos, he explained, "is the name given by most astronomers to the sphere whose center is the center of the earth and whose radius is equal to the distance between the center of the earth and the center of the earth."[2] Most Greeks believed in an Earth-centered universe. They thought the sun, moon, planets, and stars moved around Earth. Archimedes mentioned several estimates of the size of the universe according to this plan. One of these was a calculation by Phidias, his father.

Archimedes mentioned another possible scheme for the universe. He said that Aristarchus of Samos had a different view: "He supposes that the fixed stars and the sun do not move, but that the earth revolves . . . about the sun which lies in the middle of the orbit."[3] Aristarchus envisioned the sun rather than Earth at the center of our planetary system. This reference in *The Sand Reckoner* is the earliest mention of a sun-centered theory in ancient Greece. Aristarchus' idea was explored again eighteen centuries later by thinkers including Nicolaus Copernicus, Galileo Galilei, and Johannes Kepler. Finally, in the sixteenth century, the idea of a sun-centered system began to be accepted.

In *The Sand Reckoner*, Archimedes calculated the size of the cosmos. He measured it as a huge sphere with its center at the center of Earth. Archimedes assumed that not more than 10,000 grains of sand would fit inside a poppy seed. He assumed that a poppy seed is not less than 1/40th of a finger's width.[4] Archimedes calculated how many tiny grains of sand would be required to fill the vast space in the cosmos. His answer in our number system can be expressed as 10^{63} or ten with 63 zeros.[5] Archimedes also devised a way to write that number in Greek notation, which was his real purpose from the beginning.

Another of Archimedes' problems likewise involved very large numbers. In *The Cattle Problem* it was not obvious at first how large those numbers would be. Archimedes sent a version of *The Cattle Problem* to his friend Eratosthenes in Alexandria. He asked Eratosthenes to give it to other mathematicians there. Eratosthenes was the librarian in Alexandria who had calculated the circumference of the earth. This challenge was to find the number of cattle in a mythological herd owned by the god Zeus. Scholars are not certain that the exact words of *The Cattle Problem* that exist today were written by Archimedes.

The problem began, "If thou art diligent and wise, O stranger, compute the number of the cattle of the sun who once upon a time grazed on the fields of . . . Sicily."[6] There were four types of cattle; black, white, yellow, and dappled. There were cows and bulls of each color.

"Understand, stranger, that the white bulls were equal to a half and a third of the black together with the whole of the yellow, while the black were equal to the fourth part of the dappled and a fifth, together with, once more, the whole of the yellow. Observe further that the remaining bulls were equal to a sixth part of the white and a seventh, together with all of the yellow."[7] No specific number is given for any of the types of cattle. The problem provides just enough information to calculate the number of cows and bulls of each color. Archimedes did not warn Eratosthenes that the smallest answer for the total number of cattle was 50,389,082.[8]

Archimedes added two final conditions to *The*

Cattle Problem. The total number of black bulls and white bulls, he said, must be a square number. A *square number* is a product of two equal whole numbers. For example $2 \times 2 = 4$, $10 \times 10 = 100$. In these examples 4 and 100 are the square numbers. A square number can be represented by points arranged in a square with an equal number of points in each row and column. In a final twist, Archimedes said that the number of dappled bulls plus yellow bulls must be a triangular number. A *triangular number* is a type of number sometimes used by the ancient Greeks. It is a number that can be represented by dots arranged in an equilateral triangle. In this array, each row is one unit longer than the previous row. Triangular numbers are 1, 3, 6, 10, and so on.

Archimedes concluded the problem by saying that if you could solve the problem you would know that people viewed you as "perfect in this species of wisdom."[9]

The Cattle Problem with Archimedes' final conditions was solved in 1965. Canadian researchers used a computer to find the answer. The calculations took the computer seven hours and forty-nine minutes. The smallest answer for the total number of cattle is a number 206,545 digits long. In 1981, the number was published in a forty-seven page printout.[10]

Only a small fragment exists of Archimedes' puzzle *The Stomachion*. Archimedes may or may not have invented this puzzle, but he did include it in his written works. For years *The Stomachion* perplexed scholars because it seemed too simple to interest Archimedes. The puzzle is a set of fourteen geometric shapes, mostly triangles. These pieces can be arranged to form a square. They can also be arranged into shapes resembling a man, an elephant, a dog, and other figures.

Recently, Dr. Reviel Netz, a historian of mathematics, proposed a different purpose of *The Stomachion*. Netz suggested that Archimedes' challenge was to determine how many different ways the pieces could be arranged into a square.

That is a far more difficult problem than making little dogs, men, and elephants from the pieces.

A mathematical field called *combinatorics* deals with how many solutions a problem may have. Netz proposed that *The Stomachion* is a combinatoric problem. In 2003, a group of

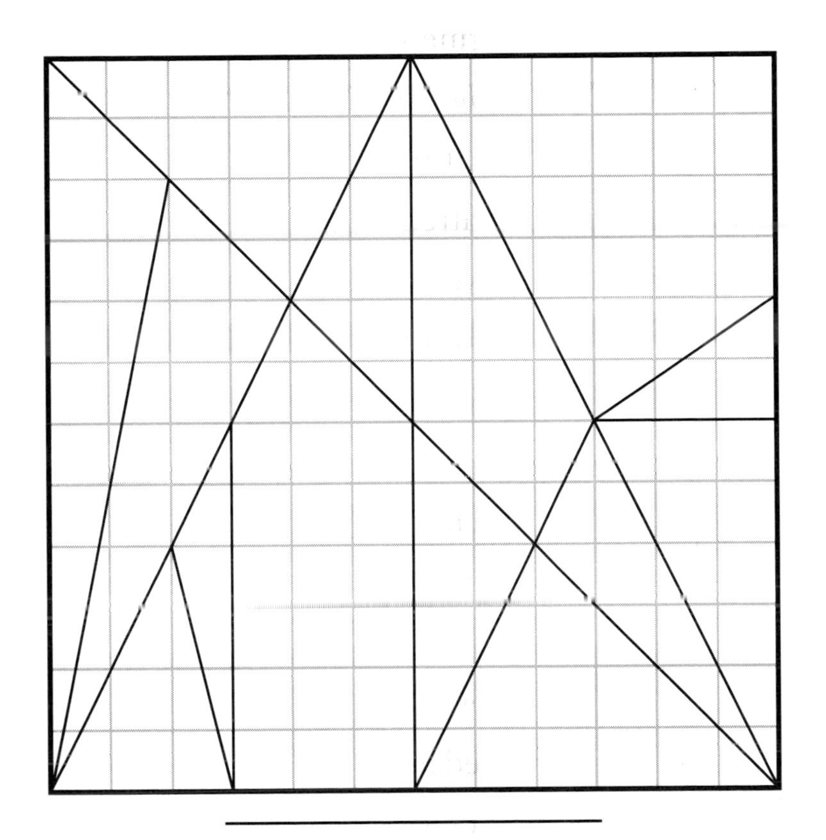

A stomachion (a tangram-type puzzle) consists of fourteen geometric pieces that can be cut from a 12 × 12 grid. Mathematicians have recently discovered 17,152 ways that these pieces can be arranged into a square of this same size.

mathematicians and a computer scientist set out to find the combinatoric answer to Archimedes' problem. They found 536 distinct solutions to the problem. By rotating the pieces and turning them over, there were 17,152 possible ways to form a square.[11]

Did Archimedes know the answer to the problem? "I am sure he solved it or he would not have stated it," said Dr. Netz. "I do not know if he solved it correctly."[12]

Archimedes' Inventions

"AND A MAN MAY WELL MARVEL AT THE inventiveness of the craftsman," the Greek historian Diodorus Siculus wrote of Archimedes. The fame of Archimedes' inventions, he wrote, "has encompassed the entire inhabited world."[1] Diodorus Siculus lived about 150 years after Archimedes.

Archimedes is credited with several inventions. He applied his tremendous knowledge of mechanical advantage in his designs. Some of his machines, including Archimedes' screw and the compound pulley, made it easier to move heavy weights. Other inventions, his planetariums, involved intricate moving parts. It is not certain if Archimedes was the original inventor of all of these devices. Ancient writers attribute them to him. However, in some cases he may have improved existing devices.

Diodorus Siculus wrote his glowing words about a machine known as Archimedes' screw. With this device, he wrote, water could be moved uphill with only a "trifling amount of labor."[2] The historian also mentions that Archimedes designed it while he was in Egypt, apparently referring to the mathematician's time in Alexandria.

Water is heavy. It weighs about sixty-two pounds per cubic foot. Splashing and leaking from containers, water can be awkward to move. The ability to transport large volumes of water with little effort was an enormous benefit in ancient times. With Archimedes' screw, farmers could raise water from streams to irrigate fields. Ancient sailors used Archimedes' screw to pump water out of ships' bilges.[3]

Archimedes' screw is a hollow cylinder.

Inside the cylinder, long curved blades wrap around a smaller central cylinder. The blades' pattern resembles a screw. The outside edges of the blades are sealed against the inside of the larger cylinder. The entire device can be turned. The cylinder is placed on a slope with its lower end in the water. As the cylinder turns, water flows in at the bottom. The water is trapped by the blades. As the cylinder continues to turn, the water is lifted by the blades until it flows out of the cylinder's upper end. In antiquity, Archimedes' screw could be powered by a person turning a crank or by a horse or ox turning a treadmill.

Today Archimedes' screws are still widely used. Massive water screws powered by electricity move thousands of gallons of liquids in wastewater treatment plants. Archimedes' screws move barley and other grains in mills. They transport fine powders in factories.

Another device credited to Archimedes is found in many modern machines. Tow trucks and construction cranes both use compound

With Archimedes' screw, water can be moved uphill.

pulleys. Compound pulleys lift elevators and open garage doors. Compound pulleys are used in a variety of machines that move heavy weights.

According to Plutarch, Archimedes used a pulley system when he impressed King Hieron II by moving the ship. Pulleys in Archimedes' weapons helped defend Syracuse.

Like levers, pulleys are simple machines. A pulley consists of a wheel with a groove for a rope, cord, or cable. A single pulley in a fixed position does not provide mechanical advantage. A single fixed pulley changes the direction of applied force. For example, if a person pulls down on a rope that passes over a pulley attached to a barn beam, the other end of the rope can lift a bale of hay up from the ground. Lifting the bale is still hard work. The person must pull down with force or weight equal to the weight of the hay.

Multiple pulleys used together provide mechanical advantage. A set of pulleys is called a *compound pulley* or *pulley system*. Compound pulleys operate on the same basic principle as levers. Pulleys use a rope rather than the rigid bar of the lever. The pin in the center of the pulley corresponds to the lever's fulcrum. Like levers, compound pulleys work by trading distance for force. With a compound pulley, a person may lift a heavy load with little effort.

Archimedes' understanding of pulleys and wheels relates to some of his other inventions. The only known book that Archimedes wrote about his inventions was titled *On Sphere-making*. Unfortunately, no copy of it exists today.

This compound pulley helps a ski lift safely carry skiers uphill.

Scholars assume that in *On Sphere-making*, Archimedes explained how he built his famous and spectacular globes. Archimedes' globes were not models of Earth. They were models of the heavens. His spheres are sometimes called planetariums.

While we do not have Archimedes' own description of his spheres, we do have an account of them from Cicero, a Roman statesman. Cicero lived about 150 years after Archimedes. Cicero had seen one of Archimedes' globes in a temple in Rome. That globe was a map of the heavens. It showed the positions of the stars and constellations. During a visit to a friend, Cicero's host showed him a second sphere made by Archimedes. At first, Cicero was not impressed. Then the host set the globe in motion. Cicero was amazed. "I concluded," wrote Cicero, "that the famous Sicilian had been endowed with greater genius than one would imagine it possible for a human being to possess."[4]

The globe was a moving model of the

cosmos. It was constructed so people could look inside it. In this sphere were "the sun and moon and of those five stars which are called the wanderers," said Cicero.[5] The "wanderers" that Cicero mentioned were the five planets that can be observed from Earth with the naked eye. They are Mercury, Venus, Mars, Jupiter, and Saturn. The Greeks called them wanderers because their movement through the sky is different from the stars. Earth stood at the center of Archimedes' sphere. The globe was mechanical. All five planets and the sun and moon circled the model Earth at different speeds. Their movements corresponded to their movements as observed from Earth.

A Roman poet wrote about Archimedes' sphere. He said that when the gods looked down and saw Archimedes' sphere, one said "An old man of Syracuse has imitated on earth the laws of the heavens, the order of nature, and the ordinances of the gods."[6]

Archimedes' spheres give us further insight into this great thinker. They show his interest in astronomy, an interest perhaps inherited from his father. They confirm that he was ingenious in using gears to make devices with moving parts. A *gear* is a toothed wheel that can interlock with other gears. There are several references to Archimedes' geared devices in ancient literature. The lost *On Sphere-making* might have provided more information about Archimedes' geared mechanisms.

An ancient shipwreck discovered in 1900 may hold clues to Archimedes' globes. The sunken ship was found by sponge-divers near the Greek island of Antikythera. The ship sank in about 80 B.C. In the wreckage was an intricate bronze instrument with interlocking gears. Altogether, the device had more than thirty gears.

Dr. Derek De Solla Price, a history of science professor at Yale University, studied the unusual instrument in the 1970s. De Solla Price concluded that the gears were part of an ancient planetarium. The mathematical ratios between the gears suggested that they were calibrated to

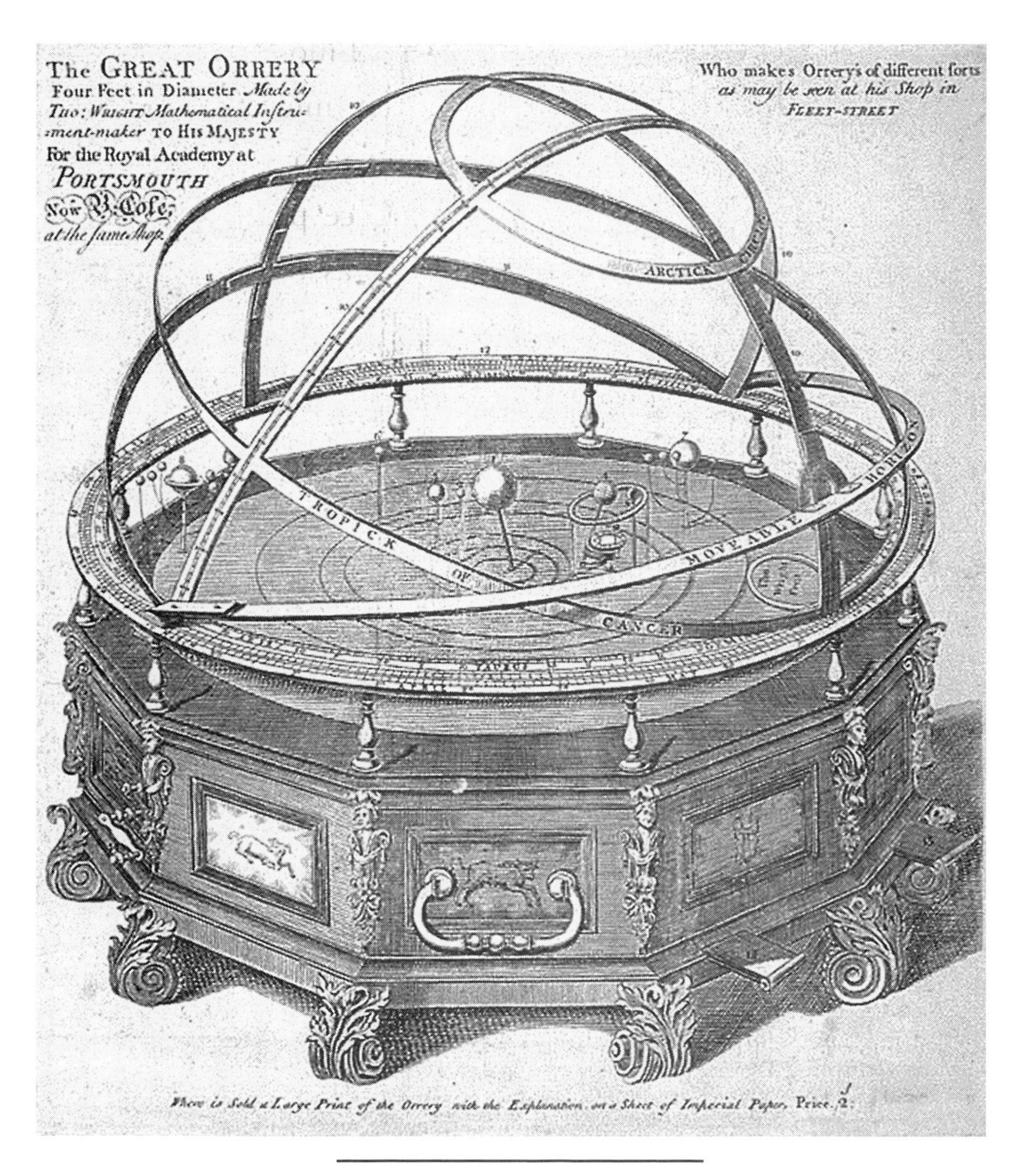

The GREAT ORRERY
Four Feet in Diameter Made by
Tho: Wright Mathematical Instru-
-ment-maker TO HIS MAJESTY
For the Royal Academy at
PORTSMOUTH
Now B. Cole,
at the same Shop.
Who makes Orrery's of different sorts
as may be seen at his Shop in
FLEET-STREET
ARCTICK
TROPICK OF
MOVEABLE
HORIZON
CANCER
There is Sold a Large Print of the Orrery with the Explanation on a Sheet of Imperial Paper, Price

An orrery is a moving model of the solar system. This orrery was designed in the 1700s. The spheres that Archimedes made may have been similar, except in his models, Earth rather than the sun was at the center of the system.

relate to movements of the sun and moon. The turning gears may have moved models of heavenly bodies. This device is known as the *Antikythera Mechanism*. De Solla Price proposed that the Antikythera Mechanism was based on the design of Archimedes' globes.[7]

The Siege of Syracuse

FOR MOST OF ARCHIMEDES' LIFE, SYRACUSE was prosperous and peaceful under the rule of King Hieron II. Hieron was a just king. He made responsible decisions for his city. Hieron expanded Syracuse's theater, built a magnificent altar for sacrifices to the gods, and added fine buildings to the city.[1] The treaty Hieron negotiated with Rome in 264 B.C. was honored. Under the terms of the treaty, Syracuse shipped grain and other supplies to Rome. In return, Syracuse was left in peace for many years while war raged between Rome and Carthage.

Rome and Carthage fought the First Punic

War between 264 and 241 B.C. When that conflict ended, Rome controlled most of Sicily. Syracuse, however, remained independent and unconquered. The Second Punic War between Rome and Carthage began in 218 B.C. Syracuse's peace was about to end.

King Hieron II died in 216 B.C. His grandson, Hieronymus, became king. Hieronymus did not inherit Hieron's wisdom. The young king changed Syracuse's allegiance from Rome to Carthage. It was a deadly decision.

Rome sent a massive army to Syracuse to seize the city. A famous general and statesman, Marcus Claudius Marcellus, led the Romans. The Roman troops planned to attack from both the land and sea. They knew that Syracuse was surrounded by a strong, high defensive wall. To scale the wall, they brought ladders. Some of the ladders were specially designed to be raised on the decks of ships. More than sixty Roman ships were in the fleet attacking Syracuse. With their large fleet of ships and many soldiers, the Romans expected to defeat Syracuse in about five days. The powerful Roman army was in for a surprise. As the historian Polybius wrote, the Romans "failed to reckon with the talents of Archimedes or to foresee that in some cases the genius of one man is far more effective than superiority in numbers."[2]

Many years earlier, King Hieron II had asked Archimedes to make weapons to protect Syracuse. In peacetime the weapons were not used. However, when the Romans attacked, the war machines were poised on and behind the city wall.

When the assault began, "immense masses of stone" bombarded the Roman soldiers on the land, explained Plutarch.[3] Rocks hurled by the Syracusans' machines "came down with incredible noise and violence."[4] In the sea, Roman soldiers rowed their ships toward the defensive wall to set up their ladders. Catapults launched boulders at them. Poles poked out of the wall and showered rocks on the ships. Boats close to the wall were "lifted up into the air by an iron hand or beak, like a crane's beak."[5] "A ship was frequently lifted up to a great height in the

An engraving done in 1740 of Archimedes planning the defenses of Syracuse.

air (a dreadful thing to behold), and was rolled to and fro, and kept swinging until all the mariners were all thrown out."[6]

Syracuse's weapons drove back the Romans. The Roman soldiers were terrified of the war machines. "If they did but see a little rope or a piece of wood from the wall," they cried out "that there it was again, Archimedes was about to let fly some engine at them." Then, "they turned their backs and fled."[7]

The Greek historian Polybius, lived just a few years after Archimedes died. Polybius may have interviewed people who were in Syracuse during the battle. He described some of Archimedes' weapons. Some machines, he explained, lowered a grappling iron or hook attached to a strong chain. The operator of the machine maneuvered the hook to attach it to a ship. As soon as the boat "was securely gripped," wrote Polybius, "the lever of the machine inside the wall would be pressed down. When the operator had lifted up the ship's prow in this way and made her stand on her stern, he made fast the lower parts of the machine, so that they would not move, and finally by means of a rope and pulley suddenly slackened the grappling iron and the chain. The result was that some of the vessels heeled over and fell on the sides, and others capsized, while the majority when their bows were let fall from a height plunged under water and filled, and thus threw all into confusion."[8]

"Archimedes uses my ships to ladle sea-water into his wine-cups," Marcellus lamented about the damage done to his fleet.[9]

After their disastrous assault, the Romans withdrew. They did not attempt another major attack. Instead, they laid siege to Syracuse. They surrounded Syracuse with their army and ships and prevented food and supplies from going into the city.

The Roman siege continued for many months. Finally the Romans detected a tower that was not carefully guarded. They prepared ladders and waited for an opportunity to invade. When the Syracusans were celebrating a feast of the goddess Artemis, the Romans moved in.

During the celebration the Syracusans were distracted by sports and wine.[10] Unnoticed, Romans soldiers climbed into the tower and onto the city wall. At daybreak Marcellus ordered the Roman trumpets to sound, announcing the invasion. Then the Roman army swarmed into Syracuse.

Marcellus was fond of Syracuse, reported Plutarch. He knew the city's beauty and wealth from the many years of peaceful relations. As the Romans invaded, Marcellus "is said to have wept much . . . when his thoughts represented to him how dismal and foul the face of the city would be in a few hours when plundered and sacked by the soldiers."[11] In that time, when a city was conquered, the soldiers ravaged it. They looted homes and temples, stealing what they wanted. They smashed and burned property they did not take. The city's people were usually killed or taken as slaves. Marcellus said that the Roman soldiers could have money and slaves. However, he said that the Romans should not "kill, misuse or make a slave of any of the Syracusans."[12]

Archimedes was in Syracuse when the Romans invaded. By every account, he died that day. In his history of the siege, Plutarch offered three versions of Archimedes' death.

First he related that Archimedes was working on a diagram for one of his problems. Totally absorbed in his work, he had not noticed the Roman invasion. A soldier commanded him to come to Marcellus. Archimedes declined, saying he could not go "before he had worked out his problem." The soldier, wrote Plutarch, "drew his sword and ran him through."[13]

In Plutarch's second version, a soldier with his sword drawn came running toward Archimedes. The soldier "offered to kill him."[14] Archimedes asked the soldier to wait as his work was incomplete. The soldier killed Archimedes in spite of his request.

Plutarch's third account had Archimedes carrying astronomical instruments to Marcellus. A Roman soldier saw him and thought he was

The death of Archimedes as represented by a nineteenth century artist. The painting shows Archimedes drawing diagrams on the ground.

carrying gold. The soldier killed Archimedes for the supposed treasure.

Another version of Archimedes' death was told by the Roman historian Valerius Maximus. In this account, Marcellus had specifically ordered that Archimedes was not to be killed.

Archimedes was at home drawing diagrams in the sand. A Roman soldier entered Archimedes' house. He was looking for loot. When the soldier demanded his identity, Archimedes was too absorbed with his problem to reply. He protected his work with his hands and said "I beg you, don't disturb this."[15] The soldier, insulted that Archimedes had not obeyed his command, killed him.

Marcellus reportedly regretted the death of Archimedes. Plutarch wrote that Marcellus sought out Archimedes' relatives and honored them with favors. Marcellus also reportedly arranged Archimedes' funeral and burial.

Archimedes had asked his friends to put on his tomb a sculpture of a cylinder containing a sphere. He asked that the monument be engraved "with the ratio which the containing solid bears to the contained."[16] The ratio he referred to was his discovery that the volume of a cylinder is exactly three halves of the volume of a sphere of the same diameter.

The Roman statesman Cicero visited Syracuse

137 years after Archimedes' death. He searched for the mathematician's grave. He found it near one of the city gates "surrounded and hidden by bushes of brambles and thorns." Cicero had the scrub cleared away and a path opened to Archimedes' tomb. A sphere and cylinder were on his monument. The engraved words beneath them were still partly visible.[17]

The Archimedes Palimpsest

A BATTERED PARCHMENT PRAYER BOOK AT the Church of the Holy Sepulchre in Constantinople, Turkey, had seen better days. Mold, fire, and centuries of use had damaged its cover and pages. Some of the book's prayers could barely be read. The prayers on the pages were handwritten in the 1200s A.D. Beneath the religious lines, faint Greek words and odd diagrams shown through.

In 1906 this prayer book was examined by a Danish scholar named Johan Ludvig Heiberg. "Eureka! I found it!" Heiberg might have shouted if he was a shouting man. Like

Archimedes in the crown legend, Heiberg had found something spectacular. The little book was a long lost collection of Archimedes' works. The book is now famous as the Archimedes Palimpsest. The word *palimpsest* means *rubbed again*. A palimpsest is a book in which the original words were rubbed off and new text written on the pages. Reusing books was not unusual before the movable-type printing press was invented in 1440.

How did Archimedes' works end up in a prayer book in Constantinople? Archimedes sent many of his manuscripts to Alexandria, Egypt. In Alexandria, his works were copied and kept on papyrus rolls. Over the years, rolls copied in Alexandria traveled to other ancient libraries. In Constantinople, starting in the sixth century A.D., there was renewed interest in ancient Greek mathematics. (Constantinople is now known as Istanbul, Turkey.) Scholars there collected and studied Archimedes' works.

By the sixth century, a more durable writing material than papyrus was in use. Parchment was made from stretched and smoothed animal skins. The name *parchment* is derived from *Pergamum*, a Turkish city where it was widely used.

In Constantinople, Archimedes' works were written in at least three codices.[1] A *codex* is an early form of book that began to appear in about the third century A.D. Information was written on individual sheets of parchment; then the sheets were sewn together.

Two codices containing several of Archimedes' works traveled to Europe. Through the centuries, his writing in them was copied, translated into other languages, and published in printed books. Renaissance thinkers including Galileo studied Archimedes from these translations. Much knowledge of Archimedes' mathematics originally came from these two codices.

The third Archimedes codex had a different history. This one was written in about 1,000 A.D. Archimedes' words may have been copied directly from papyrus rolls onto these parchment pages. About two hundred years later, this book suddenly had a new use.

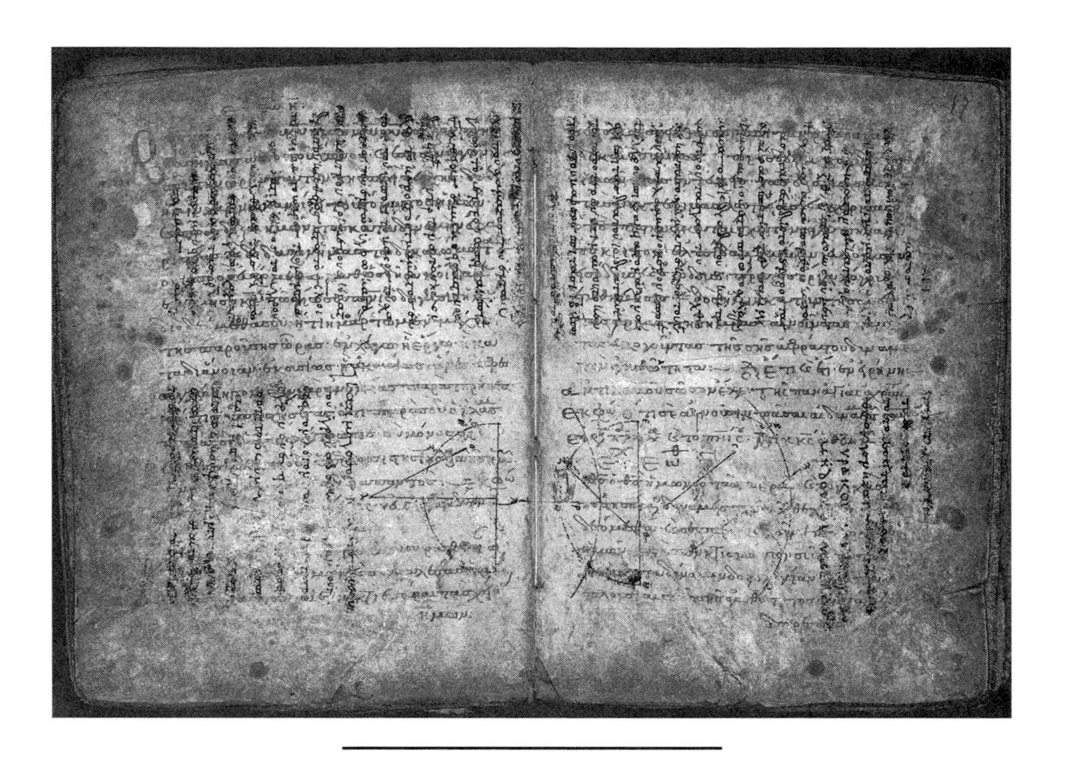

The Archimedes palimpsest. This page of the palimpsest shows Archimedes work "On Floating Bodies" written in Greek. Archimedes' words appear in the vertical lines because the original pages were twice the size of those in the palimpsest. When the original book was made into a palimpsest, it was taken apart and the pages were turned and folded in half. The prayers are written across the original Greek text.

In the 1200s, Christian religious groups wanted prayer books more than mathematics books. This was probably when the codex became a palimpsest. Archimedes' mathematics book was taken apart. The ink was scraped off the pages. The original parchment sheets were cut in half.

Prayers and instructions for religious rituals were written in fresh ink on the parchment. Finally, the pages were sewn together to make a new book.[2] Archimedes' words were barely visible beneath the prayers.

The new prayer book traveled to a monastery near Bethlehem in Palestine. It apparently stayed at the Mar Saba monastery for centuries. Monks there recited prayers written in it.[3] In the 1800s the palimpsest returned to Constantinople to the monastery's mother church. In 1899 the little book was at the Church of the Holy Sepulchre. On an inventory list, someone noted that the prayer book was a mathematical palimpsest.

Johan Ludvig Heiberg, an Archimedes expert, heard about the palimpsest and went to Constantinople. "Big Literary Find in Constantinople" read a headline on the front page of the *New York Times* on July 16, 1907. When Heiberg examined the palimpsest he saw that it was Archimedes' work. Heiberg diligently studied the palimpsest using a magnifying glass. He carefully copied what he could read. As he deciphered the ancient text, he found unexpected treasures.

The Archimedes Palimpsest contains the only existing copy of some of Archimedes' works. Almost all of an extraordinary manuscript, *The Method*, is in it. In *The Method*, Archimedes showed how he combined mathematics and physical considerations.[4] *The Method* helps mathematicians understand how Archimedes developed many of his theorems. The palimpsest contains other treasures. *On Floating Bodies* was written on its pages. Part of *The Stomachion* is there too. The palimpsest is the earliest existing Archimedes manuscript.

Heiberg was able to decipher and copy much of the palimpsest's text. However, many words were concealed in the binding. Other sections were obscured by the prayers. Some pages were missing. Heiberg's work was published and greatly expanded modern knowledge of Archimedes.

The palimpsest remained in the church library for a few more years. Beginning in 1914, most of Europe was entrenched in World War I.

The palimpsest disappeared. Who took it and where it went is not known. In the late 1930s it was in France, privately owned by a collector. For most of the twentieth century, little was heard of the Archimedes Palimpsest.

Recently, the Archimedes Palimpsest returned to public view. Its French owners offered it for sale. On October 29, 1998, the Archimedes Palimpsest was sold by Christie's Auction House in New York City. An anonymous billionaire purchased it for two million dollars.

The new owner entrusted the palimpsest's care to the Walters Art Gallery in Baltimore, Maryland. Scholars from around the world are working together to study it. With modern technology, these scientists can read words and see diagrams that were hidden from Heiberg. Over the next few years, the palimpsest will be carefully taken apart and each of its individual sheets conserved. Digital images and chemical analysis will help scholars and scientists learn more about the book and its remarkable author.

"This is the missing link between us and the

A portrait of Archimedes from an antique engraving.

diagrams that Archimedes drew in the sand," said William Noel, curator at the Walters Art Gallery.[5] The Archimedes Palimpsest is yielding new insights into one of the most original thinkers of all time. In the coming years we will know even more about Archimedes than we do today.

In the introduction to *The Method*, Archimedes

explained why he described his procedure. “I am convinced that it will prove very useful for mathematics,” he wrote. “In fact, I presume there will be some among the present as well as future generations who by means of the method here explained will be enabled to find other theorems which have not yet fallen to our share.”[6]

This brilliant mathematician and scientist might have been thrilled if he knew that generations twenty-two hundred years later still study his mathematics and learn from his works.

Activities

Activity One: Sing a Song of Pi

Pi is the symbol for the relationship between the circumference of a circle and the circle's diameter. Pi is an irrational number—it cannot be expressed as a fraction. More than a trillion decimal places of pi are known.

Some people, like Hiroyuki Goto, have memorized many places of pi. Goto recited the first 42,195 digits of pi in nine hours. You can memorize the first twenty-four decimal places of pi.

Start with a familiar song. "Mary Had a Little Lamb" works well. Instead of singing the word to Mary, sing the digits of pi. It goes like this:

Three point one four one five nine,
Two six five,
Three five eight,
Nine seven nine three two three eight
Four six two six four three.

If you practice the song, you will soon know the first twenty-five digits of pi.

Activity Two: Equilibrium

In his book *On the Equilibrium of Planes*, Archimedes demonstrated the law of the lever. A lever is a simple tool in which a bar turns on a support called a fulcrum. Archimedes showed that if the distance from the fulcrum times the weight of an object on one side of a lever was equal to the distance from the fulcrum times the weight of an object on the other side of the lever, then the lever would balance.

You will need:

- A flat ruler
- A fat highlighting marker
- A piece of tape
- A couple of tablespoons of flour
- Pennies

Position the marker underneath the ruler at exactly the marker's midpoint. If the marker is six inches long, you will tape it under the three inch line. That way three inches of ruler will extend in each direction. Some rulers have a little extra length at the ends. Consider this when finding your center point. Tape the marker under the ruler at its mid-point. Your ruler and marker are now a type of lever.

Spread a tablespoon or two of flour on a smooth surface like a countertop. The flour provides a little friction for your lever. Set the lever in the flour. The ruler should balance.

Place pennies on the end of the ruler. One penny each the same distance from the fulcrum will balance the lever. Place a penny at one end, and another penny half way between the other end and the fulcrum. What happens? Now place two pennies at the halfway point. Your lever should balance again.

Mathematically you can show this relationship by multiplying weight times distance. One penny times three inches equals three. Two pennies times one and a half inches also equal three.

You can experiment by putting different numbers of pennies at different points on the ruler.

Activity Three: Archimedes' Principle

Archimedes' Principle states that an object submerged in a liquid is buoyed up by a force equal to the weight of the liquid displaced. You can see this principle at work in this kitchen experiment.

You will need:

- A glass measuring cup that hold 2 cups or more.
- A tall glass. The glass must be taller than the length of a stick of butter.
- A one quarter pound stick of butter. The butter can stay in its wrapper.
- Cold water

Make sure the inside of the measuring cup is clean and dry. Set it on a flat surface. Fill the glass to the brim with water. Carefully set the full glass inside the measuring cup.

Lower the quarter pound of butter into the water. Make sure you do not splash the water or put your fingers in the glass. As you lower the stick of butter, water will overflow the glass. When you release the butter it will float. The butter is buoyed up by a force equal to the weight of the water it displaced.

From this experiment you can see that butter is lighter than water.

If you measure the water you will see that the quarter pound of butter displaced a little less than one half cup of water.

Chronology

Circa 734 B.C.—Syracuse founded by Greeks from Corinth.

306 B.C.—King Ptolemy I becomes king of Egypt. Ptolemy I founds Mouseion and library in Alexandria.

Circa 287 B.C.—Archimedes born. This date is uncertain, but Archimedes was reportedly 75 years old when he died in 212 B.C.

285–246 B.C.—King Ptolemy II rules Egypt. Attracts scholars and intellectuals to Alexandria. Expands collection of papyrus scrolls in library.

Circa 270 B.C.—Hieron II becomes King of Syracuse.

264–241 B.C.—First Punic War between Rome and Carthage.

Circa 250 B.C.—Archimedes studies in Alexandria; the exact date is uncertain. Sometime during Archimedes' adult life, he wrote at least thirteen works.

218–201 B.C.—Second Punic War between Rome and Carthage.

216 B.C.—King Hieron II dies.

214 B.C.—Roman armies led by Marcellus attack Syracuse. They are held back as the city defends itself with war machines designed by Archimedes.

214–212 B.C.—Siege of Syracuse. Romans besiege the city for two years before they successfully invade.

212 B.C.—Roman army led by Marcellus invades Syracuse. Archimedes is killed.

200–118 B.C.—Polybius. Polybius described the Siege of Syracuse in his *Universal History*.

106–43 B.C.—Cicero, Roman statesman and orator. Cicero wrote about Archimedes and visited his tomb.

45 B.C.–120 A.D.—Plutarch. Plutarch's writing includes descriptions of the siege of Syracuse.

Circa 1000 A.D.—Several of Archimedes' works handwritten into parchment codex.

Circa 1200 A.D.—Archimedes' mathematical text scraped off parchment; book remade as a prayer book—The Archimedes Palimpsest.

1906—Archimedes Palimpsest identified and studied by Johan Ludvig Heiberg.

1998—Archimedes Palimpsest sold at auction for two million dollars.

Chapter Notes

Chapter 1. "Treasures of Scientific Knowledge"

1. E. J. Dijksterhuis, *Archimedes* (Princeton: Princeton University Press, 1938), p. 15.

2. Plutarch, *The Lives of the Noble Grecians and Romans: The Dryden Translation* (Chicago: Encyclopedia Britannica, 1952), p. 252.

3. Dijksterhuis, p. 15.

4. Ibid., p. 9.

5. Catherine B. Avery, ed., *The New Century Classical Handbook* (New York: Appleton-Century-Crofts, 1962), p. 904.

6. Plutarch, p. 253.

7. Ibid., p. 254.

8. T. L. Heath, ed., *The Works of Archimedes* (New York: Dover Publications, 2002), p. 151.

Chapter 2. The Son of Phidias

1. Catherine B. Avery, ed., *The New Century Classical Handbook* (New York: Appleton-Century-Crofts, 1962), p. 1045.

2. David Randall-MacIver, *Greek Cities in Italy and Sicily* (Oxford: Clarendon Press, 1931), p. 141.

3. Paul Cartledge, ed., *The Cambridge Illustrated History of Ancient Greece* (Cambridge, England: Cambridge University Press, 1998), pp. 322–323.

4. Robert Garland, *Daily Lives of the Ancient Greeks* (Westport, Conn.: Greenwood Press, 1998), p. 58.

5. Cartledge, p. 105.

6. E. J. Dijksterhuis, *Archimedes* (Princeton: Princeton University Press, 1938), p. 10.

7. Plutarch, *The Lives of the Noble Grecians and Romans: The Dryden Translation* (Chicago: Encyclopedia Britannica, 1952), p. 252.

Chapter 3. Alexandria and Mathematics

1. Charles Freeman, *The Greek Achievement: The Foundation of the Western World* (New York: Viking, 1999), p. 352.

2. James Gow, *A Short History of Greek Mathematics* (New York: Chelsea Publishing Company, 1884), p. 194.

3. Graham Shipley, *The Greek World After Alexander 323–30 B.C.* (London: Routledge, 2000), p. 241.

4. John Boardman, Jasper Griffin, and Oswyn Murray, eds., *The Oxford History of the Classical World* (Oxford, England: Oxford University Press, 1986), p. 341.

5. Theodore Vrettos, *Alexandria: City of the Western Mind* (New York: The Free Press, 2001), p. 40.

6. J. J. O'Connor and E. F. Robertson, "How Do We Know About Greek Mathematics,"

<http://www-gap.dcs.st-and.ac.uk/~history/HistTopics/Greek_sources_1.html> (April 2, 2004).

7. Gow, p. 194.

8. Thomas L. Heath, ed., *The Thirteen Books of Euclid's Elements* (New York: Dover Publications, 1956), vol. I, pp. 153–154.

9. T. L. Heath, ed., *The Works of Archimedes* (New York: Dover Publications, 2002), p. ixix.

10. Ibid., p. 99.

11. Ibid., p. 233.

Chapter 4. The Law of the Lever

1. T. L. Heath, ed., *The Works of Archimedes* (New York: Dover Publications, 2002), p. 189.

2. Ibid.

3. Ibid., p. 192.

Chapter 5. "Eureka!" Archimedes' Principle

1. Vitruvius, *Ten Books on Architecture* (Cambridge, England: Cambridge University Press, 1999), p. 108.

2. Ibid.

3. Ibid.

4. Ibid.

5. Ibid.

6. Marshall Clagett, "Archimedes," in Charles Coulston Gillispie, ed., *Dictionary of Scientific Biography* (New York: Scribners, 1973), vol. 2, p. 213.

7. Vitruvius, p. 108.

8. Ibid.

9. E. J. Dijksterhuis, *Archimedes* (Princeton: Princeton University Press, 1938), p. 375.

10. Ibid.

11. Ibid., p. 376.

Chapter 6. Circles and Spheres

1. Plutarch, *The Lives of the Noble Grecians and Romans: The Dryden Translation* (Chicago: Encyclopedia Britannica, 1952), pp. 253–254.

2. E. J. Dijksterhuis, *Archimedes* (Princeton: Princeton University Press, 1938), p. 223.

3. Ibid., p.180.

4. Ibid., pp.141–142.

5. Plutarch, p. 254.

Chapter 7. Math at Play

1. E. J. Dijksterhuis, *Archimedes* (Princeton: Princeton University Press, 1938), p. 362.

2. Ibid.

3. Ibid., pp. 362–363.

4. T. L. Heath, ed., *The Works of Archimedes* (New York: Dover Publications, 2002), p. 227.

5. Marshall Clagett, "Archimedes," in Charles Coulston Gillispie, ed., *Dictionary of Scientific Biography* (New York: Scribners, 1973), vol. 2, p. 222.

6. "The Cattle Problem," *Greek Mathematical Works*, trans. Ivor Thomas (Cambridge, Mass.: Harvard University Press, 1941) Volume II, pp. 203–205. Found at <http://www.mcs.drexel.edu/~crorres/Archimedes/Cattle/Statement.html> (April 8, 2004).

7. Ibid.

8. “The Cattle Problem Solution (1st part),” <http://www.mcs.drexel.edu/crorres/Archimedes/Cattle/Solution1.html> (April 8, 2004).

9. “The Cattle Problem,” *Greek Mathematical Works*, trans. Ivor Thomas (Cambridge, Massachusetts: Harvard University Press, 1941) Volume II, pp 203–205. Found at <http://www.mcs.drexel.edu/~crorres/Archimedes/Cattle/Statement.html> (April 8, 2004).

10. “The Cattle Problem Solution (2nd part),” <http://www.mcs.drexel.edu/~crorres?archimedes/Cattle/Solution2html> (April 8, 2004).

11. Gina Kolata, “In Archimedes’ Puzzle, a New Eureka Moment,” *The New York Times*, December 14, 2003, p. 1 and p. 46.

12. Ibid.

Chapter 8. Archimedes’ Inventions

1. Diodorus Siculus, *Bibliotheke*, Book V, 37.3–4. trans. C. H. Oldfather, *Library of History*, vol. 1, Loeb Classical Library (Cambridge, Mass.: Harvard University Press, 1933). Found at <http://www.mcs.drexel.edu/ crorres/Archimedes/Screw/SourcesScrew.html> (April 5, 2004).

2. Ibid.

3. E. J. Dijksterhuis, *Archimedes* (Princeton: Princeton University Press, 1938), p. 21.

4. Cicero, *De Re Publica*, Book 1, Sections 21–22. trans. Clinton W. Keyes, *Cicero De Re Publica, De Legibus*, Loeb Classical Library (Cambridge: Harvard University Press, 1929) <http://www.

mcs.drexel.edu/~crorres/Archimedes/Sphere/SphereSources.html> (April 2, 2004).

5. Ibid.

6. Claudian, *Shorter Poems*, "Archimedes' Sphere," trans. M Platnauer, *Claudian*, vol. II, Loeb Classical Library (Cambridge, Mass.: Harvard University Press, 1922) <http://www.mcs.drexel.edu/~crorres/Archimedes/ Sphere/SphereSources.html> (April 2, 2004).

7. Richard Sanders, "Was the Antikythera an Ancient Instrument for Longitude Determination?" *21st Century*, Spring 2003. Found at <http://www.21stcenturysciencetech.com/articles/Spring03/Antikythera.html> (November 9, 2004).

Chapter 9. The Siege of Syracuse

1. David Randall-MacIver, *Greek Cities in Italy and Sicily* (Oxford: Clarendon Press, 1931), p. 133.

2. Polybius, *Universal History*, book VIII, trans. Ian Scott-Kilvery, *The Rise of the Roman Empire* (New York: Penguin Books, 1979). Found at http://www.mcs.drexel.edu/~crorres/Archimedes/Siege/Polybius.html> (April 5, 2004).

3. Plutarch, *The Lives of the Noble Grecians and Romans: The Dryden Translation* (Chicago: Encyclopedia Britannica, 1952), p. 252.

4. Ibid., p. 253.

5. Ibid.

6. Ibid.

7. Ibid.

8. Polybius, book VIII, p. 6.

9. Ibid.

10. Plutarch, p. 254.

11. Ibid.

12. Ibid.

13. Ibid. p. 255.

14. Ibid.

15. Valerius Maximus, *Memorable Doings and Sayings*, Book VIII.7.ext7. trans. D. R. Shakleton Bailey, *Memorable Doings and Sayings*, vol ii, Loeb Classical Library (Cambridge: Harvard University press, 2000), <http://www.mcs.drexel.edu/~crorres/Archimedes/Death/Histories. html> (April 5, 2004).

16. Plutarch, p. 254.

17. Cicero, *Tusculan Disputations*, Book V, Sections 64–66, trans. Michael Grant, Cicero—On the Good Life (New York: Penguin, 1971). Found at <http://www.mcs.drexel.edu/crorres/Archimedes/Tomb/Cicero.html> (April 5, 2004).

Chapter 10. The Archimedes Palimpsest

1. E. J. Dijksterhuis, *Archimedes* (Princeton: Princeton University Press, 1938), p. 36.

2. William Noel, Richard Leson, Reviel Netz, Lynn Wolfe, and Joe McCourt, "The Archimedes Palimpsest" (Baltimore: The Walters Art Gallery, 1999). Found at <http://www.thewalters.org/archimedes/palimpsest9.html> (April 2, 2004).

3. Ibid., "Archimedes Palimpsest—History." Found at <http://www.thewalters.org/archimedes/past3.html> (April 2, 2004).

4. Ibid., "Comments by Dr. Reviel Netz," The

Method. Found at <http://www.thewalters.org/archimedes/netz4.html> (April 2, 2004).

5. William Cannon, “Archimedes Unbound,” *American Scientist Online*, July–August 1999. Found at <http://www.americanscientist.org/template/AssetDetail/ assetid/15726?&print=yes> (April 9, 2004).

6. Dijksterhuis, p. 315.

Glossary

Anthesteria—An ancient Greek festival celebrated in the spring.

buoyancy—The ability of objects to float.

Carthage—Ancient Phoenician state in north Africa.

circumference—The line bounding a circle.

city-state—An independent state made up of a city and the territory around it.

commensurable—Proportionate or with a common factor.

cosmos—The universe.

cylinder—A solid figure with two equal parallel circular bases and straight sides.

dappled—Marked with spots. An animal with spotted coloring.

density—The ratio of the mass of an object to its volume.

diameter—A straight line that passes from one side of a circle to the other through the circle's center point.

displace—To take the place of.

equilibrium—A state of balance.

fluid—A liquid or gas. A substance that can flow.

force—The cause that puts an object at rest into motion.

fulcrum—The point on which a lever bar pivots.

geometry—The branch of mathematics that deals with the properties and relations of points, lines, shapes, and solids.

hydrostatics—The field in physics dealing with liquids at rest.

immerse—To place completely under a fluid such as water.

incommensurable—Not proportionate or without a common factor.

lever—A simple machine that consists of a rigid bar that pivots around a fixed point.

mechanics—The field in physics that deals with objects in motion.

myriad—An indefinitely large number—10,000 to the ancient Greeks.

palimpsest—A writing material that has been erased and written on again.

papyrus—Writing material made from the papyrus plant, a tall reed that grows in Egypt.

parchment—Writing material made from animal skin, usually from sheep or goat.

pi—The ratio of the circumference of a circle to its diameter.

plane—A flat surface on which a straight line joining any two points on it would lie.

planetarium—A mechanical model of the solar system.

polis—An ancient Greek city-state.

polygon—A closed figure bounded by straight lines.

postulate—An assumption used as a basis for mathematical reasoning.

pulley—A grooved wheel that a rope or cord can pass over.

Punic Wars—Three wars fought between Rome and Carthage, 264–241 B.C., 218–201 B.C., 149–146 B.C.

radius—A straight line from the center to the circumference of a circle or sphere.

Rome—Capital and center of the Roman Empire.

siege—A military operation in which a fortified place is surrounded by an attacking force.

sphere—A solid figure with every point on its surface equidistant from its center point.

theorem—A proposition that can be proved with accepted truths.

volume—The three-dimensional amount of space occupied by an object.

Further Reading

Bendick, Jeanne. *Archimedes and the Door to Science*. Bathgate, N. Dak.: Bethlehem Books, 1995.

Keating, Susan. *Archimedes: Ancient Greek Mathematician*. Broomall, Pa.: Mason Crest Publishing, 2002.

Perkins, David. *Archimedes Bathtub: The Art and Logic of Breakthrough Thinking*. New York: W.W. Norton & Company, 2000.

Stein, Sherman. *Archimedes: What Did He Do Beside Cry Eureka?* Mathematical Assoc. of America, 1999.

Zannos, Susan. *The Life and Times of Archimedes*. Bear, Del.: Mitchell Lane, 2004.

Internet Addresses

Archimedes Home Page
http://www.math.nyu.edu/~crorres/Archimedes/contents.html

Archimedes of Syracuse
http://www-groups.dcs.st-and.ac.uk/~history/Mathematicians/Archimedes.html

Archimedes Palimpsest
http://www.thewalters.org/archimedes/

Index